Sons of the Soil

by

Michael Schoepf

Foreword

Every family, indeed every individual, is a story. Each life has a beginning, a middle and an end and includes moments of joy, drama, tragedy, conflict, triumph and defeat, all the elements of a good novel. Most of those stories, however, never show up in history books, much less find their way to a movie or television screen. Many of them even go untold, save for being passed down from generation to generation by word of mouth, altered with each re-telling. Sadly, a number of them undoubtedly perish with time. Perhaps that is part of the natural order of human existence, but I'm not willing to passively accept that.

What you are about to read is the story of not one, but two typical immigrant families that came to the United States at almost the exact same time, leaving behind everything they knew in Europe and following the matching dreams of hopefully building a brighter future. For over a hundred years, these families followed parallel courses. Some members of each succeeded, some didn't, all in varying degrees. I'll let you judge each character. I simply want to present in words a picture of what I guessed their lives to be.

No project like this story is the work of solely one individual. A number of people served as inspirations for this narrative, and an even larger number helped in so many ways to make it a reality by providing fascinating facts and enrapturing stories. A list of those folks, as complete as I can make it, appears at the end. To those whose names I may have inadvertently omitted, I apologize in advance.

Lest anyone assume that I take those closest to me for granted, I most of all want to thank my absolutely adorable wife Bev, my talented daughter Maria and my not-so-shy son Tony for being the biggest part of my life. They are the reason I do the things

I do, and I don't want them to forget that. Perhaps someday, one of them will write my story. In the meantime, read and enjoy...

Sons of the Soil

July brought the annual humid stifling heat to Clayton County, Iowa. Some of its sticky tentacles poked their way through the cracks in the clapboard walls of a two-bedroom house in the village of Clayton Center. After midnight, the air hung heavily everywhere. Despite the darkness, Johann Schoepf sat at his customary chair in the kitchen area, more concerned with what was going on inside his head than what was happening outside.

Raised as a man of faith in his native Weissenstadt, Bavaria, Johann felt that status threatened. The previous eighteen months had taken its toll on him and his family. Save for having found steady employment, nearly none of the reasons for which he had left his fatherland had become a reality. In fact, the opposite had happened. Could this be what God had intended for him and his loved ones, he wondered? Was he being tested? Or was he simply damned?

A little over two years earlier, Johann made a decision he agonized over for months. He was a shoemaker by birth and by trade. In fact, for at least three generations prior to his, the Schoepfs were the only shoemakers in Weissenstadt, and business, though not prosperous, was steady. There was enough demand for new shoes and repairs that Johann, his father, also named Johann, and one of his younger brothers, Tomas, also stayed busy. After the family patriarch died in 1839, the Schoepf cobbler shop continued to operate at a brisk pace.

In 1843, Johann's mother Christianna died at 50, and the youngest Schoepf boy, David, a lad of ten, was ready to learn the shoemaking trade. Though Johann didn't realize it at the time, those events coincided with the beginning of the end of the Schoepf family as shoemakers.

In the mid-1840's, hard economic times hit Bavaria, along with other parts of Europe like Ireland. In all of what was to eventually become Germany, money became scarce, and there was precious little of it to spend in discretionary fashion. Germanic people knew little and cared less about the devastating potato famine that had infected Ireland and caused hundreds of thousands of Irish to flee to America. Nor did it matter to Bavarians that large numbers of Russian Jews and Italian laborers were also enduring difficult times and seeking westward refuge. All Johann knew was that business had steadily slowed, and he knew the reason for that.

Shoes were constructed of leather and, sometimes, a portion of wood. A long-time skilled cobbler such as Johan and his ancestors and Tomas, learned to read leather and wood. They learned through instruction and experience how to tell a supple yet durable piece of potential shoe leather from an inferior one. They also learned to recognize the tight grain of wood that made the best heels for boots, heels that would last under the constant pounding of feet bearing the weight of a human body. Unfortunately, those same skills were demanded of farmers who maintained their own tack needed for farming, and farmers made up a large portion of the Schoepf family business.

Normally farmers were too busy working to raise crops and livestock to provide the actual footwear for themselves and their families. They knew that the comfortable and durable shoes and boots made and maintained by the Schoepfs were a convenience that enabled them to spend more time in their immediate livelihood. After all, Johann realized, why spend unnecessary time getting ready to farm when one could actually be tending to crops and livestock instead.

While leaving the shoemaking and repair to the Schoepfs, farmers also knew the value of maintaining much of their own farming equipment. Until the invention of the steel plowshare in 1839, farmers spent much of their winter time honing wooden plowshares from tree stumps they had removed from their property. For that reason, they knew, as the Schoepfs did, that a tight grain, usually found low on the trunk, was the hardest wood and made the best plows. Because steel plows were not yet readily available in Europe, farmers around Weissenstadt still crafted their own wooden plows.

Nor was the knowledge of quality leather the exclusive domain of the shoemaking Schoepfs. Those same farmers who so capably made their own wooden plows were equally skilled at working with leather. After all, they had bridles, harnesses and saddles to maintain, and that was something they had always done. Hence, when economic times became difficult, farmers were quick to embrace the idea of repairing their own shoes rather than spending rarely possessed money to buy new ones.

Johann knew that shortly the family business would be incapable of supporting his family, the one that Tomas would soon be certain to start, and, eventually the one David would likely have. Shortly after New Year's Day in 1852, he decided to do what so many other Bavarians had already done. He would move his wife and four children to the United States.

Iowa, Clayton Center in particular, was the only American destination Johann considered. A number of his former neighbors in Weissenstadt had already gone there. One family, the Schmidts, had emigrated several years earlier and settled in New York. After a short stay there and in Ohio, they found themselves in Iowa as part of a growing German population in Clayton Center and neighboring Elkader, the Schmidts had started a sizable farming operation and a brewery and were rumored to be considering other business ventures. Certainly, Johann thought, Iowa seemed to offer an opportunity for him and his family. He made plans to divest himself of his piece of the family business and depart for Iowa as soon as spring arrived.

On April 12, 1852, Johann, his wife Katherine and their children, Anna, Elizabeth, Maria and the year-old Johann boarded the *Uhland*, at Bremen, bound for New Orleans, Louisiana. They wore several layers of clothing, both for warmth and so that the amount of luggage needed would be minimal. Included in the Schoepf party was Katherine's sister, Anna Ruckdaschel. Katherine and Anna's parents had been deceased for over ten years, and Anna seemed to have little future in Weissenstadt. Though almost twenty-five years old at the time, Anna had never had any suitors. Johann thought that was because she was quite plain to look at, rather homely in fact. He reasoned, however, that she would earn her fare by being of great assistance to her older sister in providing care for four children, including a newborn.

At first look, the *Uhland* was a majestic sight to inlanders like the Schoepfs. It was a three-masted, square-rigged wooden vessel that was supposedly the largest German ship of the time. From her launching in 1847, she was assigned exclusively to make the Bremen to New Orleans and back run several times each year. The *Uhland* looked large enough to provide safe passage to a new life some five thousand miles distant and adequately comfortable to make the journey tolerable. Those hopes were soon dashed.

From the trip's outset, the typical springtime waters of the North Atlantic, swelled regularly by icy polar winds, made for a jostling ride at best. As the northern invaders buffeted the ship, the Schoepf family, along with most of the other immigrants, stayed in their rooms clutching the frames of their bunk beds to avoid being tossed to the floor by the rolling vessel. Nausea was a constant companion. Three weeks passed before the waves subsided and the motion illness passed. That left some six weeks remaining before their arrival in New Orleans. Johann hoped that the worst of the voyage was over. Again he was mistaken.

With the smoothing of the ride, the shipboard rats, present from the outset, seemed emboldened. Perhaps they, too, thought Johann, had needed some time to acclimate themselves to the choppy passage. Now, fully accustomed to the accommodations, they appeared more numerous and assertive. They went where they pleased, ate whatever they wanted, sometimes even off plates still in use and left their droppings everywhere. As a result, most passengers ate little, and a number became ill. Some, a total of eight in all, died before the *Uhland* reached land in Louisiana. Finally, on June 12, after precisely nine weeks at sea, the ship docked in New Orleans to the relief of 330 passengers who had completed the trip. Departure for shore was not to be quick, however.

Six days aboard the *Uhland*, anchored inertly in the New Orleans harbor, made Johann even more impatient than had the tedious trip across the Atlantic. All passengers had to be examined for communicable diseases and any other debilitating infirmities. Each, except for small children, would be questioned. What is your name? When were you born? Where are you from? Why have you come to the United States? What do you intend to do here? Have you ever been convicted of a crime of any kind? Do you have any relatives here? Where in the United States do you intend to go? These questions took very little time to ask and answer, Johann noted. The real reason for the lengthy delay, he learned, was to verify the absence of any major health epidemics. Some five years prior, he was told, a ship of Irish immigrants had brought with them an outbreak of typhoid fever to Canada. As a precaution, those infected, as well as those who travelled with them, were quarantined on a large island in the St. Lawrence River until the danger passed. While they were there, many died. Since that time, immigrant ships in all ports were treated with utmost caution.

On the morning of June 18, 1852, the six Schoepfs and Anna Ruckdaschel were finally allowed to depart the *Uhland* and enter the city of New Orleans. Johann wasted no time in booking passage for them on a riverboat bound north up the Mississippi River for a place called St. Paul, with numerous stops along the way, including one near Clayton Center, Iowa, his destination of choice. Again, he was certain that good fortune was about to shine on him and his family.

The *Ruby Eldrey* trudged its way up river from New Orleans at an even slower pace, but at least the paddle wheeler provided none of the unwanted churning or sickening experiences of the *Uhland*. Amusement was in short supply, so Johann took notice of the man who stood at the front of the boat frequently measuring the depth of the water and calling out his measurements. Johann noticed that his announcements often caused the man standing in the small house, who seemed to be in charge of the vessel, to spin a large wheel in front of him to steer the ship. The course never followed a straight line, instead wandering almost as far back and forth across the water as it went upstream. Eventually, Johann concluded that was because the river had a sandy bottom and the undercurrent was constantly changing its depth.

Nearly three weeks later, after countless stops to unload and load freight and passengers, the *Ruby Eldrey* steamed ever closer to Guttenberg, Iowa, where Johann and his family would depart for Clayton Center, a half-day overland away.   As the riverboat moved wearily north, Johann marveled at the beauty of the Mississippi River shoreline. Both sides, Wisconsin on the right and Iowa on the left, he learned, were lined with trees on rolling hills as far as he could see in either direction. That sight was reassuring to him, for it looked much like the terrain around Weissenstadt and gave him the feeling that perhaps Iowa would be more than suitable as home for the Schoepf clan. At least it looked familiar.

Johann relaxed even more upon discovering that a dozen or so other Weissenstadt natives who had made the same journey with the Schoepfs had been correct. Through correspondence with relatives already in Guttenberg, they were informed that the city was almost totally German in nativity and that German, more than the English Johann was learning only slowly, was by far the dominant language. In a new country that looked and sounded like the old one, a new start should be easy to attain, he reasoned. Confident he had made the right choice in uprooting his family, Johann purchased stagecoach tickets for all and set off for Clayton Center.

Only a day after arriving in the sparse but bustling village of Clayton Center, Johann found work as, of all things, a shoemaker and a general purpose carpenter, thanks to Karl Schmidt, the oldest of the Bavarian brothers who had ventured to America and prospered. He remembered Schmidt looking at him through undersized glasses and speaking through a bushy mustache that hardly ever moved.

"My brothers and I expect only the best effort from all those in our employ," he said somewhat sternly after barely meeting Johann. Schmidt then sat silently for an awkward minute or so, studying Johann for a reaction. "I can already see that you are a worker," he finally commented. Then he sat silent long enough to see the quizzical look on Johann's face. "Your forearms and your hands," Schmidt said. "They are thick from the work they are accustomed to doing. Your chest, too, is thick. Only a man of constant hard labor has those qualities. I believe you will do well." With that, Johann had found a job and was ready to build the future he had barely begun to dream possible. Yes, he told himself enthusiastically, Iowa was a very good place to be.

For over a year, Johann continued to believe in himself and his good fortune. In that time, he found that he had something of a gift for carpentry. He thoroughly enjoyed it, particularly when something he built was complete, and he knew it was both functional and durable. He often told Katherine that many of the things he had made for the Schmidts would last far longer than he would. At first she would laugh and smile with him. By late summer of 1853, she was not so quick to do so, he noted.

The Indian summer sun was only beginning to set as Johann returned home one evening the year before to find an unfamiliar single-horse carriage parked in front of the house. Upon entering the dwelling, he found Katherine and a man he recognized as Dr. Weiss, the local medical practitioner, seated at the table. Anna was pouring coffee for them, and they looked somber. Johann immediately shifted from curiosity to concern, and he was the first to speak.

"What is happening?" was all he could think to say.

"Our son is ill," was Katherine's simple response. Johann knew that his son Johann had been "out of sorts", as Katherine and Anna had said on a few occasions for the past few weeks, lacking in his customary two-year-old energy bursts, but the father had no idea that anything was seriously amiss.

"How do you mean, ill?"

"He has a fever, Johann," Dr. Weiss stated. "I've been here since early this morning, and I haven't been able to break it. If it doesn't give in soon, I'm afraid his little body will start to shut down. It's already frail." Johan sat for a moment in stunned silence.

"Why is this?" he finally asked.

"No one really knows," answered the doctor. "Sometimes it just happens," he added resignedly. Johann shifted his gaze to Katherine, looking for hope that wasn't there, either. By early morning, the despair became reality. Little Johann died peacefully in his sleep. Four weeks later, his three-year-old sister, Maria, followed him in the same fashion, leaving Johann the father unable to sleep as winter started to creep into northeast Iowa.

As Johann Schoepf sat at his table looking for answers that would not arrive, his wife Katherine sat next to him with a hand placed softly and motionlessly upon his. He didn't outwardly acknowledge her presence, but he knew she was there. They had hardly spoken to each other at all in the week since Maria's funeral. Johann wanted to know her thoughts, but he didn't ask because he was afraid of what they might be. He feared she might blame him for bringing their family to a place where they might all perish. Why not, he told himself. That idea might actually be the truth. So they sat in silence, not even looking at each other.

Over the Christmas season of 1853, Johann and Katherine tried to put two tragic deaths behind them and focus on their remaining children, Anna and Elizabeth. They spent as much time as they could at the Clayton Center Lutheran Church, hoping silently that God would comfort them and that being among friends would somehow ease their pain. Though helpful to some degree, that strategy stopped working as January set in. By that time, both Johann and Katherine were separate vessels bound only by a common sea. Though sociable with their children, they rarely talked between them. Their few exchanges were courteous but unemotional.

By spring of 1854, Katherine was obviously physically wasting away. Anna had reported to Johann on many occasions that her sister was skipping meals on a regular basis and that Katherine was spending more and more entire days in bed. She was also increasingly uncommunicative with everyone in her life. On numerous occasions, Johann implored his wife to get her life together for the sake of her two daughters. Those pleas went ignored.

In mid-July, Johann Schoepf spent another night at the kitchen table rather in the bed of his wife. Again, he was filled with fear and doubt. Perhaps Iowa was a bad idea, he wondered. Maybe he and Katherine were being punished for his decision to come here.

"Some people fear the darkness, you know." Johann heard Anna's voice penetrate his thoughts. " I can see you don't."

"I'm losing her, Anna."

"You already have."

At sunrise on July 12, Johann rose from his unwanted post at the table and went to look in on Katherine. She never awakened again.

1855

Forty miles north of Clayton Center, scattered snowflakes floated on the slight chilly breeze. The driver of a wagon accompanied by a woman and two small boys ambled toward the Wexford Immaculate Conception Church along the Mississippi River eight miles south of Lansing in the northeastern corner of Iowa. The wagon driver, John Healy, figured that a little extra moisture, even on April 8, Easter Sunday, could only help to ensure that the coming farming season would be well worth the effort, as had the previous two. John was right to leave Canada, he knew. He sometimes wondered, though, why he had taken so long to make that decision.

Eight mostly difficult years had passed since John, his wife Bridget and their newborn son William had left their native Ireland seeking another existence abroad. They were typical immigrants of the Great Potato Famine in that they were hoping for a better life than what Ireland offered, but they weren't sure where or how to find one. They just wanted to go somewhere, anywhere, and hope for a new chance, so the three of them boarded a ship in Dublin that was bound for Quebec in Canada.

The trip to Quebec was expected to take just over six weeks, but rough seas and an outbreak of typhoid fever among passengers and crew extended its duration to nearly nine weeks. Once in Canada, the ship was forced to halt at a place called Grosse Ile and wait at anchor for six days in quarantine. After that, the Healys were forced to remain at Grosse Ile for three months until gaining permission to enter the city of Quebec. All that time, John and Bridget watched as countless of their fellow Irish succumbed to the deadly typhus, and they hoped that somehow, it would not touch them or their vulnerable infant son. Unknown to them, the death toll due to typhus for that year alone at Grosse Ile would eventually number some 5,000. Several thousand others became casualties in other places.

In mid-September, John Healy and his family were finally granted medical permission to enter the city of Quebec and, hopefully, their future. With another couple that had survived the trip from Ireland, they found a two-bedroom apartment in a rundown section of the city, and the men found work in a foundry that made parts for railroad engines. The work was exhausting, dangerous and low-paying, the norm for Irish in Quebec. The immigrants were generally considered to be an inferior race of people characterized by sloth and drunkenness. The natives of the city thought by and large that the Irish were useful only in the role of human machines whose existence was merely functional and therefore tolerable.

A year after John's departure from the Emerald Isle, his brother Michael, two years younger, left the homeland for the United States, Boston in particular. There Michael put to work his considerable charm, energy and literacy to land a position as a law clerk. It was a low-paying job, for sure, but one with promise of a future. After nearly two years, Michael had turned his renown in the Boston legal society into a role as a non-commissioned officer in the U.S. army cavalry and had been deployed to the southwestern part of the country. His communication skills and strong Catholic faith made him an exemplary chaplain during his tenure.

While living in Quebec, John received an important letter in the fall of 1852. It came from his youngest brother James who had departed Ireland in 1851 with a group of some 1,200 parishioners of Father Thomas Hore of Wexford. Father Hore had led a contingent of three vessels, including the *Loodiana*, on which James had travelled, to New Orleans in a place called Louisiana. From there the group had voyaged north up the Mississippi River looking for a suitable location to start an Irish colony and parish. After stops in Texas and Arkansas, where no affordable land was found, the party continued on until it reached St. Louis. At that point, Father Hore proceeded alone in search of a new home while the others remained in St. Louis. After three months of consulting with church officials up and down the Mississippi Valley, Father Hore announced that he had found 1000 acres of farmland for sale in a place called Allamakee County, Iowa, a place bordered on the south by Clayton County, Iowa and the east by Wisconsin. To the north lay Minnesota.

Father Hore's long-awaited announcement in St. Louis was greeted less-than-enthusiastically. By that time, many of the voyagers had grown weary of awaiting news of an uncertain future and had found a meager but steady lifestyle in St. Louis. Only eighteen families, a total of about 100 people including the unmarried James Healy, went to Iowa with Father Hore.

According to the letter James had sent to John, Iowa was a future that none of the Healy boys had ever dreamed of. The farming was difficult, to be sure, for the river bluff country, though fertile, needed to be cleared, and the land was not particularly flat. That same land, though, according to James, seemed to grow crops well almost by accident. After all, James had stated in his communication, he was prospering at farming, a field about which he knew very little. He urged John to consider doing likewise.

Not only was John Healy easily convinced to go to Iowa, but Bridget was, as well. The future they had hoped for was obviously not going to happen for them in Canada, where discrimination against their origins would always be an insurmountable barrier. As they saw the situation, they had absolutely nothing to lose by going to Iowa. They left within weeks and accepted James' invitation to stay with him until they could locate some land to purchase. Bridget's foresight in saving money she earned in doing laundry for others for several years made a trip by rail, as well as buying land, a genuine possibility.

For John and Bridget Healy, six-year-old William and three-year-old Thomas who had been born in Quebec, life in Iowa happened fast. Shortly after New Year's Day in 1853, he found a 100-acre tract of land for sale and snapped it up. It was a bit expensive, James told him, at $1.60 an acre, but it was partially cleared and had a sod house on it. The Healys could move right in and begin farming right away and could therefore expect a harvest income in the fall.

By the end of 1853, John Healy knew that James had been right. A man could make money in Iowa either because of or in spite of his efforts, it seemed. Like James, John not only had little prior experience in farm work, but he didn't fancy himself as farmer material. In that year alone, John Healy's farm yielded as much income as had five years of toil in Quebec.

1854 was even more bountiful for John and Bridget Healy and their sons. During the previous year, John, with some help from James, cleared trees from more of his farm, thus allowing for the production of even more crops. John also added some dairy cows and some chickens and made plans to expand into hog or sheep production for 1855. The expression "luck of the Irish" took on a whole new meaning for John Healy.

Economic prosperity and its anticipated continuation was not the only thought that fueled John Healy's happiness as he guided the family wagon to the log church next to the Mississippi River on Easter Sunday. Later that day, his brother Michael would be arriving by coach in Lansing, and an unexpected family reunion would occur. John didn't know what Michael's plans for the future were, but he hoped that that there was a chance of his brother joining him and James in the growth of Allamakee County. With that possibility in mind, he glanced up the hill to the west, where the foundation of a new limestone church was being dug, smiled toward Bridget and his sons and went into the church.

A sacred Lord's Day, coupled with Father Hore's penchant for providing the spoken word made for a longer-than-usual homily, as John had expected. After all, John recalled, Father Hore had somehow convinced nearly 1,200 people to follow him for 6,000 miles from Ireland to Iowa with no guarantees of a better life. Few other men, priest or layman, possessed that kind of persuasive talent. A man who could do that was worth listening to, thought John.

Just before the conclusion of the service, Father Hore made an announcement that caught John's attention. On the second Sunday in May, the priest had said, catechism services would begin for all parish children aged five years and up. That meant that William would begin receiving religious instruction then, something that was important to the Healys. Despite the difficult times they had endured in Ireland and in Canada, their strength of faith never abandoned them. Both John and Bridget felt that belief in the Catholic church and its teachings had indeed sustained them when they had every reason to give up. Now they knew they would have help in imparting those teachings to their sons and any future children they would have.

After church, John Healy escorted his family back to the family farm two miles south of the church. He then saddled one of the horses and rode the ten miles to Lansing where the nearest stage station was located. As he passed the church, James joined him. Michael's stage would be arriving from La Crosse, Wisconsin, at two o'clock. That should allow the two men time, John calculated, to return to the Healy farm in time for John to complete his newly acquired milking chores in their usual fashion. As his horse trotted casually along the dirt road, John noticed that the snowflakes had disappeared and the sun was driving away the few puffy clouds that remained. It was a grand day, John told himself, and it was about to get better. Others can have Ireland and Canada, he thought excitedly. He had Iowa.

All the way into Lansing, John wondered what his brother had become in the nine years since they had last seen each other in Ireland. Michael was always the thinker, John recalled, the one who was always looking ahead and making plans. In impoverished Donoughmore in County Cork, though, that type of thought was generally a waste of time, for it led to no future. For the majority of the parishioners there, life was simply to be survived for awhile. The real rewards, according to the church, would come in the next life. Sometimes John wondered if the reason that Irish people held such strong belief in an afterlife is that they suffered so much in the present one. Michael, his brother, was not one of those to be content with letting life happen to him now in exchange for future reward. No, John knew, Michael was a doer. If he didn't like something, he set about to change it. John wondered if he were still that way.

For the first mile or so, the brothers Healy rode without speaking. Then James broke the silence.

"Do you suppose we will even recognize Michael ?"

"I should hope so," John replied. He was well aware that the three brothers bore a very similar body structure to each other.

All were short, stocky and displayed a rubicund visage around hazel eyes. Their hair was brown with a tint of red. All in all, they looked like all the Healy men they ever knew. Spotting another one, especially among a small group of passengers at a stagecoach station, shouldn't be difficult.

"Have you any idea what he plans to do now that he's through with the army?" asked James.

"I'm hoping he'll see fit to settle here," John answered. "This is a good life, and there's enough for more to enjoy as well."

"True, true enough," acknowledged James. "That would be a good thing." Then the silence resumed.

Only a few people were about at the stage station in Lansing, and Michael Healy was indeed easy to spot. In addition to the customary Healy physique, he was the only one adorned in a military uniform. After some robust salutations and hugs, Michael explained that the decorations in the uniform identified him as a lieutenant and that during his service in Texas, he served as a chaplain. It was a particularly difficult role, he added, as a yellow fever outbreak had scourged south Texas at the time. He said he couldn't begin to count the number of unfortunate men, women and children to whom he had been entrusted to administer last rites, as priests were in short supply. He was glad to be shed of that duty, he added.

After Michael rented a horse-and-carriage rig at the livery stable, the brothers started their southward journey. Michael had agreed to stay with John and his family for a few days. That did his older brother's heart good, John thought, for it would give him time to see if he could convince Michael to settle in the Lansing area. By the time they had all reached their destinations, the sun shone brightly, the air was nearly warm and the snowflakes of the morning were merely a memory.

After supper, John and Michael sat at the kitchen table and caught up on each others' lives for the past nine years since each had found his separate way of escaping Ireland. While John and Bridget had gone directly from Dublin to Canada, Michael had found work on a ship bound for Liverpool, England, and eventually made his way to Boston, Massachusetts. Once there, he said he was fortunate enough to find that his ability to read and write, rare among Irish at the time, enabled him to find work as a legal clerk in a prestigious law office. His professional contacts in Boston helped him gain a commission as an officer in the Army at a time when most enlistees were assigned to the infantry. In five years of military service, he had distinguished himself and saved some money as well. Michael, it seemed, still had the ability to look into the future and make it work for him.

"You're blimey lucky to be here," was Michael's emphatic response to John's story of surviving the winter of typhoid fever on Gross Ile and years of discrimination and poverty in Quebec. "And it seems you've done well here," he added. "Iowa certainly doesn't look like the Ireland we left."

"So would you consider staying here?"

"I might," Michael said through a smile. "I just might at that." They downed another draught of ale and went to bed.

For the next three days, Michael stayed with John and Bridget and the boys, William and Thomas. He arose early each morning and helped John with the milking. Then he assisted in the examination of the harnesses, plows and other equipment that was necessary for the spring planting season that was about to begin in earnest any day. John noticed his brother was nearly "farm fit" as he put it, and he attributed that to Michael having lived a military lifestyle for several years. The arduous life of an Iowa farmer was physically not that much more demanding from that of a soldier on the frontier, John guessed.

During that same three days, Michael captured the fascination of William, the older of John's two sons. Will, as he was called, constantly implored Michael to relate stories of his time spent in Texas. The young man's insatiable appetite for information about a place and people so far away and apparently somewhat different in culture seemed somewhat of a waste of time to John, but he knew that Will was simply indulging a boyish curiosity. He only hoped that Michael was not annoyed by the young man's constant barrage of questions. Michael assured John regularly that he was not.

On Wednesday evening, Michael announced that he would be leaving the next morning after chores were finished. His announcement carried both sad and good tidings for John. Michael explained that while he had to go to St. Louis by riverboat to attend to some personal business for a few days, he would not be leaving Lansing until Saturday morning. In the meantime, he planned to spend time in the area looking for land to buy. It seems, he said, that his brothers had impressed upon him the abundance of opportunity that lay waiting in northeast Iowa, and he planned to partake of it as soon as he could. Before Michael left on Thursday morning, he and John agreed to meet for a late supper in Lansing on Friday night so Michael could update John on his search. Michael also asked John to relay the news to James and to invite him to supper in Lansing on Friday as well. As Michael's horse and buggy left the Healy farm and turned onto the River Road north toward Lansing, John felt a sense of contentment he had never felt before.

On Friday night, Michael had great news for the Healy brothers. He had indeed found some land about three miles west of the Wexford Immaculate Conception Church. He had agreed to pay $2.40 an acre for a nearly cleared 120-acre plot. The price was a bit steep, John thought, but the land was almost devoid of trees and, thus, ready for farming. Even at that price, John reasoned that Michael should have no problem in making a profit for the upcoming farming season. Toward that end, he offered his brother whatever assistance he could provide in the form of labor and equipment. John knew that, if accepted, that offer would put more responsibility on nine-year-old Will, but he knew Will would relish the opportunity to help his favorite uncle. By the time the three Healys parted that evening, all seemed set in their world. Ireland was nothing but an inspirational bad memory. Iowa was life to them.

1864

"NO!" Anna Schoepf barked at her husband on a winter evening. "That is not a good thought." The tears that had been welling in her eyes spilled over onto her cheeks. Her husband Johann simply stared blankly at her. Then he turned away from her and began to pace the small living room of their small house on the south edge of Clayton Center, Iowa. A moment later he turned to face her.

"There's little choice," Johann said, trying to sound as self-confident as he could.

"Why?" Anna answered.

"We came to this country to make a new life for ourselves, " Johann explained, "a better life. Look around you, Anna." He waved his arms as he continued. "Do you see anything here that is better than it was in the Old Country? Do you?" He paused, knowing full well that he was too emotional at the moment. After calming himself, he went on. "Anna, my darling Anna, don't you see that after over ten years in America, we are no better off than we were in Weissenstadt? Worse even. We own nearly nothing, no land, no business, nothing. At least in the Old Country, I had a shoemaking business to call my own. Here in Iowa, our name is not on anything."

"Is that more important than life to you?" asked Anna, her cheeks still wet with tears. After a minute of reflection, Johann replied.

"It's a part of life, a very important part. I want you and our children to have more than I've been able to provide."

"I'm happy with what we have."

"I'm not. I'm nearly an old man, Anna, and I've done nothing to provide for the ones I love after I'm gone. This is my only chance to do something truly important for all of us."

"You could be killed trying!" Anna exclaimed. "Haven't we experienced enough death since we came here?" She made a good point, Johann knew. Two of his children, along with his first wife, Katherine, who was Anna's sister, lay buried in the Clayton Center Lutheran cemetery. They had died soon after the family's arrival in Iowa.

"It is a chance I must take," Johann said firmly. Then Anna sat pensively before speaking.

"I am not in favor of this," she said. "But if you feel this is something you must do, so be it. I will remain here and take care of our children. That is my duty as your wife. But I'll have you know that I will not rest easy for a minute until you come home. I would ask of you one favor, though."

"And what is that?"

"That you think about this overnight. By morning, you have my blessing to do whatever it is you think you must. And I shall not complain."

"Agreed."

In the morning, Anna Schoepf awoke alone in their bed.

A sharp February breeze darted down the Turkey River valley in northeast Iowa, nipping randomly at some objects in its path, including Johann Schoepf as he walked briskly northward on the west side of North Main Street in Elkader. In response, Johann simply pulled his woolen coat up toward his running nose and watering eyes. Then he quickened his pace, less due to the weather and more because he was anxious to reach the point of no return.

When he arrived at the building with "119" painted on the glass above the door, he paid scant attention to the superbly crafted oak door itself. Normally, he might have admired its workmanship, the same type of pride and care he and his brothers learned from their father, also named Johann, in making shoes in Weissenstadt in the Old Country. Today, though, he felt no such need or desire. He had a far more important matter on his mind.

Johann entered the building into a lobby area and closed the door behind him. Though he hadn't walked in snow, he stamped each foot twice to remove any that he had picked up on the way.

"How may I help you, sir?" Johann turned his attention from his boots to the source of the question. Before him at a table sat a smallish woman in her late thirties or early forties with wire-rimmed glasses perched on the end of her nose.

"Yes," replied. "I'm Johann Schoepf, and I'm here to see Mr. Proctor. "

"Have you scheduled an appointment?"

"No, no I haven't," answered Johann. "But I saw him last week, and he asked me to return this week. "

"It's just past nine on a Monday morning. You don't waste much time, do you?" Johann saw a smile appear just below the nose supporting the glasses. "I'll tell him you're here." With that, she rose and walked to an office in the back of the building.

Momentarily, a tall, rather thin man in a stylish suit, including a vest and bow tie, came out to the waiting area and extended his hand.

"Mr. Schoepf, it's a genuine pleasure to see you," he said through a smile. Johann was warmed to hear his last name pronounced correctly so that it rhymed with "pep". Most people said it so that it rhymed with "cough". Johann reassured himself by thinking that a man like Rueben Proctor, who took care to pronounce a difficult German name correctly was a man worth doing business with. At least Johann hoped so.

Unlike the front door, two signs of Rueben Proctor's prosperity did catch Johann's attention as he followed the attorney into his private office. Johann noticed first the charcoal gray wool suit that fit the tall, thin man well. It didn't hang limply in places the way cheaper cuts did on the lanky. It was a suit unseen in Johann's world.

After Johann was ushered into Proctor's office the attorney closed the door behind them and bade Johann to sit. He then filled a coffee cup and offered some to Johann, which he accepted.

Before either man could say a word, Johann's eyes fell upon the massive desk before him. He guessed it to be some nine feet long and nearly five feet deep. Nearly every square inch was covered with books and papers. The edges, though, captivated Johann. The two-inch high wood was ornately carved in fine detail as far as he could see. Rueben Proctor obviously possessed the fine taste of a man often mentioned as a likely candidate for public office.

"I assume you're here to discuss the matter we talked about last week," Proctor stated. Johann simply nodded his head, partly because he knew his command of English couldn't compare to the attorney's but more because he wanted to hasten toward the meeting's conclusion. "Have you spoken to your wife about this?" Again, Johann nodded. "And what are her thoughts?"

That question took Johann's mind where he didn't want it to go. He and his wife Anna had carried on a generally strained and often heated conversation for over a week, ever since Johann had broached the subject. Stinging tears had flowed freely from both of them. In the end, they had reluctantly agreed that the choice was Johann's and that she would support it as best she could.

Almost twelve years earlier, Johann had left Weissenstadt, Bavaria, with a wife Katherine, two sons, two daughters and Katherine's sister Anna. The grueling seafaring voyage on the *Ulland* took a toll. Everyone took ill with the chills. From New Orleans north up the Mississippi River, travel proved no less arduous. Iowa seemed unreachable, but still the promise of the New Country burned brightly.

To support his brood, Johann accepted work with the Schmidt Brothers, who owned a considerable amount of farmland in Clayton County in northeast Iowa. The Schmidts, too, had come to Iowa from Weissenstadt only a few years earlier, with intermittent stops in New York State and Ohio. Within two years, Johann's children Johann and Maria became sick and died of a fever. Katherine soon followed, leaving Johann with daughters Anna and Elizabeth to raise alone save for help from his sister-in -law. Five months later, he married Anna, and they began a family by adding another Johann and Friedrich to their group. It seemed like a fresh start, but it wasn't.

Ten years later Johann's dreams had become a mere flicker, nearly extinguished. He still owned no land and felt beholden to the Schmidts for the food on his family's table, the clothes on their backs and the roof over their heads. Though they were more than fair as employers, Johann saw himself as a farm implement, not much different from a plow or harrow, to be used only when needed and ignored otherwise. When worn out, he would likely be cast aside, most likely to be cared for by his children, who would repeat the process. No, that's not what Johann wanted for himself, Anna and their children. That's not why he came to the United States. His latest plan would change that. It would be his legacy.

"She is worried," Johann said to Rueben Proctor.

"She has reason to be," the attorney replied. "This is certainly a dangerous venture, especially for a man of your age. Tell me again, how old are you?"

"Is it important to know?" Johann asked.

"It could be," Proctor countered. "After all, wisdom generally accompanies years."

"What are you trying to tell me?"

"That perhaps after thinking about my offer and talking about it with your wife, you've realized how risky this arrangement can be. Maybe you've seen how much you have to lose."

"Sir," Johann interrupted. "I have very little to lose. I have been in this country for almost twelve years, and I have little to show for why I came here. I own no land and have no means of getting any. If I don't do this, I'll have nothing to give my family except the memories of a man who worked himself to death to make others rich. That's not why I left Weissenstadt."

"So you're certain you want to do this?" Proctor asked.

"Yes, sir," Johann replied promptly.

"Alright, Mr. Schoepf, I'll make the arrangements. Just so you know, you'll need to be in Dubuque on February 11. That's a week from this coming Thursday. I'll provide travel fare and a letter of introduction. Once I receive confirmation that you've done what you promised, I'll see that your family receives the sum of $500. Do you agree to those terms?"

"Yes," Johann said and nodded. This is what he had come for.

"Mr. Schoepf, you have done my family, particularly my son, a great service, and I truly appreciate it. I can only hope that this war will soon end, and that you return safely to your family." He stood and reached to shake Johann's hand, an offer Johann eagerly accepted.

With that encounter, Johann Schoepf, an almost 47-year-old carpenter and farm laborer from Clayton Center, Iowa, took the first step toward becoming a private in the 27th Iowa Infantry. He would enlist in place of Rueben Proctor's son Lorenzo, who had been drafted. In exchange, Johann would receive $500, enough to tide his family over until his return. In the meantime, the $13 a month he would earn as a soldier could be set aside to finance a new beginning for the Schoepf clan after the war ended. Johann knew that if he survived military service, he might be able to provide a fresh start, one which involved land ownership, which he saw as the key to prosperity in America. He had heard of something called the Homestead Act of 1862 that provided for that, along with special privileges for veterans of military service. As he saw his current situation, he had very little choice but the one he had just made.

Until his business with Rueben Proctor, Johann had no interest what the people of Clayton County called The War Between the States. Oh, he knew that it had something to do with slavery. He also heard something about whether states had a right to leave the country, but none of that mattered to him. In the past week, all of that changed.

On his way back home, Johann detoured to the village of Clayton Center, nearly six miles east of Elkader, to the homestead of his employers, Karl and Joseph Schmidt. The Schmidts had always treated him fairly, and he had done them likewise. He owed them more than just a notification of intent to quit his job of almost twelve years. They deserved an explanation, and he would give them one. When he arrived, he found Wolfgang, generally the more amiable of the two, in the massive barn tending to a cow that had just given birth. Both mother and calf appeared to be doing well.

The meeting with Wolfgang resulted in a pleasant surprise, one Johann was sure that Wolfgang's brother J.B. wouldn't have offered. J.B. was the numbers man of the Schmidt operation and often seemed aloof from those who did his bidding, even his five brothers. No, Johann was sure J.B. wouldn't have offered Johann the opportunity to leave his family in a company-owned house while he served in the military. Wolfgang asked for one favor in return. Johann listened intently, something he had done all morning.

Wolfgang told Johann that John Schmidt, the youngest of the brothers at 18, had enlisted in the 27th Iowa Infantry, the same unit Johann would be joining. John was scheduled to be in Dubuque on February 11, the same day as Johann. Wolfgang proposed that out of a sense of loyalty for Johann's diligent service to the Schmidt family and more because of a need for someone to watch over John while he was away, that the Schoepf family would be allowed to remain in the farmhouse they lived in and to help out the Schmidt families with domestic chores. Johann readily accepted. Not only would his family not have to move within the next week-and-a-half, but the arrangement would allow for his pay as a soldier to be largely saved for a new beginning for the Schoepfs when Johann returned. What started out as a day of suspense and hope had turned into a day of fruition.

The trip home passed quickly. So lost in his thoughts was Johann that he scarcely noticed the cold wind that had plagued him in Elkader. With every step of his horse, he was giddy with his good fortune. He thought of nothing but how the good news he had gathered would ease matters at home. The part about not having to move might stop the frequent flow of tears running down Anna's face of late. At least she and their children would have a place to live during his absence.

Johann's prediction came true. Anna's face beamed at most of her husband's report. Johann knew she still hated the idea of him leaving to face danger for any amount of time. He also knew that she would always fear for his safety, for she had repeatedly told him so. He admired her putting up a good front for the sake of the entire family.

At mid-morning of February 11, Johann Schoepf and John Schmidt sat on the outdoor bench of the freight station in Elkader awaiting a wagon train from Lansing, 45 miles to the north that would take them and seven other Clayton County men to Dubuque to be mustered into military service. When the caravan arrived shortly before 9:30, they discovered that it was already full of nearly 30 other recruits from Allamakee County to the north.

Conversation with those men revealed that most of them were from the community of Rossville.

"Can't be many men left in that town," remarked Johann.

"Most of 'em's Irish," said John. "I doubt Rossville will miss them, except for the saloon owners." Johann knew whereof John spoke. Almost from the time he had first arrived in Clayton Center, Johann heard many of the residents talk of a group of Irish settlers who had come at about the same time and settled forty or so miles north near a place called Wexford. Those people had made the same journey northward up the Mississippi River that Johann and his family had made. The Irish, however, were unable to find a place that would accept them until a priest of some sort found some cheap land in Allamakee County, land which consisted primarily of tree-covered sandy hills, the kind which was difficult to prepare for farming and just as hard to farm afterward.

Johann had also heard that the Irish were a hard-drinking lot, and Catholic besides. That made them quite different from the stoic Lutherans by whom Johann and others in the area were surrounded. Beer was a staple of nearly every German meal, but it wasn't consumed to excess as the Irish supposedly did with whiskey and some sludgy concoction called stout ale. No, they didn't seem like the type of people with whom Johann would care to associate any more than necessary. He also felt a need to see young John Schmidt didn't do so, either.

Fort Dubuque was teeming with military activity when Johann and John arrived a little after noon. Because of the time of day, the new recruits, numbering about a thousand, were gathered in a large room for lunch. Although the hearty fare consisted of a beefsteak, boiled potatoes, corn and bread, Johann was sure that that wasn't the normal menu. After lunch, the fresh enlistees were lined up and made to pass through a line of men in white coats for what seemed to be a visual physical examination. That was followed by an individual exam involving a cold stethoscope, numerous questions and a considerable amount of prodding and poking by gnarled fingers.

"Good shape for, shall I say, one of the older soldiers," the man in the white coat stated. "How old did you say you are?"

"Over thirty," Johann answered. He was afraid he would not be mustered in if his real age of nearly forty-seven were known. He didn't rightly know if there was a maximum age for military service in the United States Army. He did know that he didn't want to lose his last shot at success on account of his age. Besides, he reasoned to himself later, he hadn't really lied.

By late afternoon, Johann and his protégé, John Schmidt, had officially passed muster and become enlisted men assigned to Company I of the 27th Iowa Infantry regiment. They, along with some fifty others, took the oath of a U.S. soldier and were directed to march to the Fort Dubuque supply depot to be issued uniforms, boots, blankets and various and sundry items, most of which were unfamiliar to the new recruits. As a former shoemaker in Germany, Johann took particular note of the boots and saw that, unlike the footwear to which he was accustomed, neither boot was designated for the left or the right foot. Instead, they were designed to fit either foot. He also noted that they seemed to come in only two sizes. After some thought, Johann concluded that that oddity of footwear probably made the boots easier to produce on a massive scale so as to outfit an army.

One of Johann's worries was the training period. His age presented him with worry about being able to perform the physical skills to keep up with the others of his unit and to do what he needed in order to survive and return to his family in Clayton Center. Within a few days, those anxieties had all but vanished. Despite his age, Johann not only held his own within the ranks of the newly enlisted, but sometimes outperformed them, especially in the areas of manual dexterity, such as loading a rifle. He guessed that perhaps that was because he had counted on his hands to support him for more years than most of his mates had been alive. Nor did the 5:30 a.m. reveille bother him, for he had arisen early to work for nearly his entire life. The daily hand-to-hand combat practice was the only part he found grueling, but he knew that might be essential for survival. In fact, Johann found that the most difficult element of basic military training was the sheer boredom of it. Day after day, he and the rest of the fresh enlistees did the same things over and over, urged to think about each one until thinking was no longer necessary. Considering that those procedures were very simple in nature, Johann figured that three months of that were certain to try his patience and wear on his nerves. He wondered if that ordeal made soldiers more than eager to fight rather than to endure more training.

In mid-May, the boredom ended. The new recruits were then supposedly combat-ready troops prepared to take on their first assignments. On a surprisingly chilly morning, they were all loaded on riverboat that began a trudge down the Mississippi River bound for a battlefront in somewhere in Mississippi. The boat ride gave Johann a chance to retrace his steps of over twelve years ago on his way from Germany to Iowa. The only change he noted was that more towns, with attendant commercial buildings and houses, had sprung up since his last passage. That was to be expected, he knew. The United States was still a growing nation, and the current war was most likely one it its growing pains. He guessed that, just like his personal life, a nation couldn't move forward without an occasional step backwards. He'd had his share of the reverse ones, he thought. What he was doing now was his way of trying to achieve what he came to America to do.

1868

Seemingly each thought in David Schoepf's head was punctuated by the sound of a small Mississippi River wave lapping gently against the hull of the *Byrle Norrell* as it snaked its way northward avoiding sawyers and sandbars on the Great River less than a day south of Guttenberg, Iowa, in April of 1868. The sternwheeler and its passengers were warmed only by the noon sun overhead on what was an otherwise nippy day.

Standing on the foredeck, David marveled at the wooded landscape on the left side of the river and wondered if his brother Johann, sixteen years his senior, would recall making the same journey in 1852. Hillsides of trees lined the Missouri side of the wide waterway, and rolling farmland filled the vista of the Illinois side. David wondered which terrain he would see farther north in Iowa and Wisconsin.

Like Johann, David had left Weissenstadt, Germany, with his family, including his wife Margarethe and their two sons and year-old daughter for reasons both like and unlike those of his older brother. Johann had left when he realized that the Schoepf family shoemaking business would no longer support the three Schoepf brothers and their families. He wanted more economic opportunity and believed that the United States, Iowa in particular, would provide that. David wanted that for his family, too, but other factors pushed him toward the same decision Johann had made.

The Bavaria in which the Schoepf brothers grew up no longer existed. Instead of being a small independent state which shared many customs and the German language with its neighbors, the country had become one of many in the process of melding together into something similar to the United States, a coalition of codependent yet independent entities. That was the stated dream of Otto von Bismarck, Chancellor of Prussia. Bismarck had just begun his efforts to form a unified Germany, and many natives, including David Schoepf were uneasy about what they had seen and heard.

Bismarck believed openly that a strong nation needed, among other things, a formidable military and a high quality network of roadways. Both of those required manpower, manpower and more manpower, even more than came forth voluntarily. Hence Bismarck used the military to fill the needs of both forces. He ordered his legions to scour the countryside rounding up any sons who were not truly needed to work the family business. Those boys, some as young as twelve, were given a choice of military service or road building, and were thus torn from their families. David Schoepf determined that his sons would face that predicament. Though his sons were currently four and five years old, he feared things would not change in the next several years. He had to escape Bavaria for that reason.

David watched his sons, five-year-old Johann, named after David's father, and four-year-old Mattias, run about the small deck of the *Byrle Norrell* and admonished them to be careful of others . He then turned his attention toward the water ahead and thought more about his situation.

"You will need to learn a new trade," his older brother had written. "In America, there is no need for shoemakers. Shoes are made by machine, hundreds, perhaps thousands, every hour. And they are sold in stores called general stores, along with food, clothing, tools and many other goods." At first those words concerned David. He knew no other trade, and, at thirty-five, wondered if he was too old to learn a new one. The next words he read in Johann's letter soothed him somewhat. "I myself," continued his brother, "found that my shoemaking abilities helped me as a carpenter. An ability to work with both hands and tools is valuable in America." David hoped his brother was right, for the future of his family could well depend upon that.

In mid-afternoon, the *Byrle Norrell* rounded a bend in the mighty river and David caught sight of a handful or so of white limestone buildings standing as sentinels on the west side of the river. He knew from his brother's description that was the village of Guttenberg, Iowa, a German name for a city where German culture universally existed, right down to the language spoken. David reasoned happily that Guttenberg, being a home away from home, would be a good place for him and his family to spend the night before going on to Clayton Center in the morning. Some authentic German food would be welcome, he thought, along with some genuine German beer.

Along the journey from Weissenstadt to Iowa, good beer is what David missed most. The few offerings he had sampled on his voyage had been either pale yellow weak concoctions or thick, syrupy almost liquid substances that were probably better suited for consumption by spoon. The former, he learned in passing, was usually hastily made in order to satisfy the growing American population's demand for beer. The latter was the favorite of mostly Irish, making it a socially questionable choice as well as being unappetizing.

From a fellow passenger on the *Byrle Norrell*, David discovered that, to no surprise, the most popular beer in the region was made by a German in St. Louis, Missouri, a city the boat had just passed nearly two days earlier. Eberhard Anheuser operated a huge and expanding brewery on the south side of the city. He and his son-in-law, Adolphus Busch combined Bavarian know-how and American entrepreneurial spirit to reach the same sort of success that David hoped to achieve for himself, Margarethe, Johann, Mattias and, hopefully, children to come. The story of the Anheuser Brewing Company reassured him that coming to America was the right move for the Schoepfs.

Guttenberg proved to be the new but recognizable and comforting haven David had hoped for on their long trip. For a time, he no longer worried about his fractured English being understood. He could speak German freely without getting quizzical looks in return and he could readily understand what was said to him. The food, too, was familiar and was prepared in traditional German family style. For part of a day, David felt as if he had never left Weissenstadt.

Early the next morning, David rose, dressed and ventured out to find the stage station in Guttenberg. There he found that the next coach to Clayton Center would depart at 10:00 that morning. That allowed more than enough time for the family to enjoy a leisurely breakfast. As they did so, David toyed with the idea of actually settling in Guttenberg. Eventually, he dismissed the notion. Perhaps someday, he thought, but for now, he determined to follow his original plan.

The four-hour coach ride from Guttenberg to Clayton Center seemed interminable to David, but it gave him time to ponder his surroundings and his immediate situation. To begin with he wondered if he was seeing the same sights that his older brother had some sixteen years earlier. Then he saw that the coach was moving even slower than had the *Byrle Norrell*. A look out the window explained why. The horses drawing the coach were pulling it gradually uphill and around curves almost constantly. Hence, the driver knew enough to conserve their energy by holding them to a stroll rather than urge them to a trot. The countryside was absolutely beautiful, David thought, even more green and rolling than that around Weissenstadt. Then he wondered how anyone could possibly clear such land, much less, farm it. It had to be more flat around Clayton, he concluded. Johann's letter didn't say so, but it did say that the farmland in Iowa was abundantly productive. He couldn't imagine any other possibility.

"Are you sure Johann will take us in?" Margarethe asked, interrupting her husband's thoughts. "After all, he does have three children of his own living at home. That would make ten of us in the house, and that seems like too many." David saw the concerned look on her face and knew he needed to reassure her.

"They are family," he said. "And family finds a way to take care of one another. And it shouldn't be for long. I'll look immediately for work and a place for us to live. Besides, our children are about the same age as Johann and Anna's. They will have much fun together, I'm sure."

"They may be family," Margarethe continued, "But you hardly know them. It has been sixteen years, you know, and only a handful of letters between the two of you. How will you even recognize Johann after all this time?"

"Trust me, I will know him. He's my brother. I will know him." David hoped that his last remark would end the conversation, for he knew that his wife had raised some very valid points.

By mid-afternoon, the stage had reached Clayton Center, and the five Schoepfs got off and readied themselves for the last leg of their journey to a new life. Johann's last letter stated that his home was on the south end of the village, a short walk for David and his family.   Only minutes after arriving in Clayton Center, the travelers found themselves at the doorstep of the Johann Schoepf home.   Anna greeted them warmly and informed them that Johann was still at work and would be home in a couple of hours.

As Anna led David and Margarethe on a tour of the house, David could see why Margarethe was concerned about space. Although the bedrooms were somewhat sizable, there were only two of them.   Anna explained that her seven-year-old William and four-year-old John could sleep in the living room with Johann and Mattias.   It would be a great new adventure for all of them, Anna had said.   David and Margarethe would then have the second bedroom to themselves.   Lizzie, David and Margarethe's one-year-old, would sleep in her parents' room, and Johann and Anna's year-old Frederick would sleep with his parents.   With the accommodations settled, David noticed that his wife seemed to relax some.

Anna brewed a fresh pot of coffee, and she and Margarethe conversed about the journey from Weissenstadt to Iowa.   David remained silent most of the time.   He preferred to save his conversation for later, knowing full well that whatever he said at the moment would likely have to be repeated to his brother later. Telling his story once was enough for him.

Around dusk, David heard the front door of the house open and instantly understood the reason for one of Margarethe's concerns.   A thin slightly stooped over man with a bald head walked in and just stood staring at the newcomers in his home.   A pair of rimless glasses perched toward the end of his nose.   His face and hands were wrinkled, and his overalls were obviously worn.   For a moment, neither man spoke.   "David?" queried the man who looked old enough to be the newcomer's father.

"Johann?" In an instant, the brothers moved toward each other and hugged hard. Sixteen years had been sixteen years, but David was sure the blood ran thick between them.

Separated but still holding arms, the two men began a conversation. "I see you have arrived safely," Johann began, his eyes lighting up as he spoke. "And your family, too?"

"Yes, yes," replied David. "We are all here. My wife Margarethe," he said, waving toward the women in the kitchen. "And little Johann and Mattias and Lizzie."

"Johann?" David's older brother asked. David merely nodded. "Well," said Johann, "It seems we have a goodly supply of Johanns around here. I just hope we can keep all of them straight." That remark drew a hearty laugh from all four adults present.

Throughout supper, the conversation focused on the arduous voyage David and his family had just completed. David noted that their experiences did indeed parallel those of his older brother and his family in 1852. He hoped the similarity ended there. David did not want to endure the loss of two children and a wife. By the time the meal ended, he was anxious to talk with his brother about getting a life started in Iowa. As the women began to clear table and prepare to wash the dishes, the men adjourned to the family room.

"It is good to see you arrived safely," said Johann. I'm sure there were times that you had your doubts about what you are doing." He paused for a moment to light a pipe. "I know I did." He paused to look into the fireplace.

"One of your letters said you fought in a war," David said. Were you not rather old to be doing so?"

"Perhaps," was the only reply.

"So what caused you to do such a thing, with a family to tend?"

"Let me answer by saying this, my brother. In America, there is one thing that is the same as it is in the New World. "Johann stopped long enough to puff on his pipe. "Land. Land is the most important thing. Those who have it are in control of their lives. Those who don't aren't."

"I don't understand," quizzed David. "How does fighting in a war have anything to do with owning land?"

"After twelve years in Iowa, I still did not have what I wanted," Johann continued. I looked into the future and saw nothing more than being another man's carpenter until I die. Then I would leave my family with nothing to call their own. I came to this country for more than that. When I had all but given up hope of changing my future, an opportunity came to me, an opportunity I couldn't pass up." Again he paused to take a puff from his pipe.

"What kind of opportunity?" David asked.

" A man in Elkader, a prominent man, announced that his son had been called to serve in the United States Army in what people around here call the Civil War. At that time, the government had the power to demand that men serve in the military so that enough soldiers could be available to fight the war. Anyone called to serve, however could send someone in his stead, and this prominent man offered the sum of $500 to anyone who would replace his son in the army. So that's what I did. I took his money and his son's place and served for two years. Then I came back to my family, $500 richer."

"But you are still here," David interjected. "And you are still doing the same thing you were doing when you left. How did fighting in a war help you?"

"As I said, I received $500 and I also earned the right as a former soldier, to claim eighty acres of extra land."

"What do you mean by extra land?'

"A year or so before I became a soldier, the government made a law called the Homestead Act that made possible for people to claim certain land as their own for no more than a small filing fee. If you live on the land and farm it for five years, it then becomes yours for no cost. So that is what I have decided to do." Again he puffed on his pipe.

"That is great news," David said, genuinely joyful for his brother. "Where is this land you plan to claim?" Johann did not answer quickly.

"Have you ever heard of a place called Nebraska?" Johann finally asked.

"Is it far from here?"

"Yes, it is. Almost four hundred miles west and south."

"Why so far?" asked a very curious David.

"Iowa land is too expensive," answered Johann. In Nebraska, I can own more land and afford to farm it as well." The two brothers sat in silence for awhile. David was thankful for the opportunity to understand what he had just heard. He wondered if this changed the plans that he and Margarethe had made. For the moment, his world had turned topsy-turvy on him. He had been counting on his brother to help him get situated in America. Johann had given no indication in his letters that he was planning to move elsewhere. David wondered if he had been somehow deceived. It mattered little right now, he concluded. So he pondered his options as he noticed that his brother had slipped into sleep.

As David saw his situation, he had three options. The first one, returning to Weissenstadt, he ruled out immediately. He had not the funds to do so, and he knew that the reasons he left it behind were just as true now as they were when he left. Accompanying Johann to this place he called Nebraska was unrealistic for the same reason. He guessed that he barely had the money for the trip and would have none left to buy land. No, he decided. That was not a possibility. That left him with only the reality of staying in Clayton or nearby Elkader and finding work until he could put together enough of a nest egg to buy land of his own. He hoped it wouldn't take him sixteen years as his brother had to do so. Ironic, he mused. We're sixteen years apart in age, we came to the America sixteen years apart, and Johann needed sixteen years to put himself in a position to own property. No, David decided, he would break the chain of sixteens.

Shortly after retiring for the evening, David found that Anna had not so much as hinted to Margarethe of the impending move of Johann, Anna and their children to Nebraska. Margarethe said that communicating such news might be more of a manly responsibility rather than information a woman should impart.

"I agree," David said. When he realized that his wife was not responding, he glanced at her to see her fast asleep. David soon followed, grateful that he would not have to deal until tomorrow with the stress he knew she would feel after thinking about the situation. It had been a long day, he concluded. Perhaps a couple of hours too long.

The following morning, David arose when he heard sounds coming from the opposite end of the house. He carefully picked his way through the slumbering bodies of children camped in the living room toward the light of the kitchen where he found Anna at work over the stove and Johann seated at the table making some sort of adjustment on a shoe.

"Old habit?" David asked.

"Old trade," replied Johann. "But fortunately not a forgotten one. How are you this morning, brother?"

"Good," replied David. "Good."

"I trust you slept well," Johann continued.

"I did," said David. "I did indeed."

"That is good to know." The elder Schoepf stated. "After breakfast, I would very much like for you to come to work with me today. I want to show you something." Johann continued to tinker with the apparently troublesome shoe in his hand.

Sunrise found the Schoepf brothers walking north on a dirt road toward the heart of the village. David was silent, waiting for Johann to reveal whatever he had in mind for him to see. He noted that even at 51, Johann was able to walk at a brisk pace. Perhaps the spring morning chill helped cause that, he guessed.

Johann led them to a huge wooden building on the west edge of the city. The wooden structure was a large as a barn, but it obviously wasn't one. The first thing David noticed as they entered the building was several work stations, each with a different project in progress. At one, a handful of men were making wooden barrels. Another featured repairing what appeared to be various farm implements. Near a large open back door, not one, but two blacksmith forges roared in the early morning air, providing heat and then some for everyone inside. Johann stopped just inside the doorway and turned toward his younger brother.

"All of this, and much, much more, belongs to the Schmidt brothers," Johann said, waving his hand over the entire scene before them. "They own several farms, a brewery and the biggest mill in Elkader," he continued. "If you decide to look for work, I would start with them. Come. Let me show you what I do." Johann then led David to a work station about halfway through the gigantic room and on the right. A number of pieces of furniture populated the area, and most of them were in a stage of repair. Again, Johann stopped to speak to his brother.

"This is my home away from home, at least for the next month," he said. "My job is to build and repair furniture for all the Schmidts' business interests and for the families themselves. 'My master carpenter' Wolfgang calls me. "

"The next month?" David queried.

"Yes," Johann said boldly. "And after that, Nebraska. That's why I wanted you with me today," he continued. I want you to see what I do, and if you like it, perhaps I could talk to Wolfgang about having you take over for me." He stopped to await a response.

"Are they good to work for?" David asked. "You know I have never worked for anyone else before."

"You worked for Papa in Weissenstadt, did you not? And Tomas? They were often stern and difficult. So was I when I was teaching you about shoemaking. You survived us, so I'm sure you can survive the Schmidts. All they ask is a fair day's work. Let me tell you something, that Wolfgang, besides being fair, is generous as well. When I went off to serve in the army, he let Anna and the children stay in our house that the company owns. All he asked in return was some household help from Anna and that I watch over the youngest Schmidt, John, who left with me. I'm happy to say that both of us returned to our families on the very same day, and none the worse for wear." David could plainly see that Johann was proud of his military service.

"Will you tell me about the army and the war sometime?" David asked.

"There's not much to tell. It was very boring most of the time. Then the confusion took over. Finally, the war was over, and we got to come home. "

"Did you fight in any battles?"

"Five of them, at least big ones. And a few small ones, too. That's when the confusion happened. Most of the time was the boredom. "

"Did you shoot at anyone?" David asked excitedly. "Did you kill anyone?"

"I shot at the enemy," Johann said. "I don't really know that I took a life, though. After I fired a shot, I ducked my head to reload without knowing if I hit a target or not. That was the best way I could think of to stay alive. Here, you can help me." He handed

David a file and showed him how to take the rough edges off a piece of wood that would soon become part of a desk, he told David.

For most of that morning, David worked with his brother. Many of the tools they used were identical or very similar to the ones they had used to craft shoes in Bavaria. David saw, too, that Johann kept his tools organized within his work area. Thus, he lost little time in searching for what he needed at any given moment. Nor did he stop to think about what he needed to do next. David could see that each task was planned while the previous one was being accomplished.

Occasionally as the brothers worked, other workers would stop by Johann's work area to visit for a moment. David observed that everyone showed noticeable warmth and respect toward Johann, and concluded that this place was a friendly place to make a living. If Johann was right, working for the Schmidts would get him and his family off to a fine start on their new life.

In late-morning, Johann excused David and told him that he should go home to talk to Margarethe. "Are you sure? Don't you need more help?" David asked, trying to conceal his joy at how his fate had turned.

"I'm sure," Johann said. "Besides, I did not bring enough lunch for two of us. Go. Go." He waved his hand toward David as he spoke.

Warming temperature and excitement made David's trip back to Johann's house both comfortable and quick. When he arrived, he found Margarethe helping Anna to feed the herd of hungry children who seemed to be everywhere.

Without awaiting an opportunity to speak to his wife, David ushered her by the arm toward the kitchen table and coaxed her into a chair. He knew he was babbling some, but he could hardly wait to inform Margarethe of the good news. Before he finished, he saw tears of joy racing down her cheeks toward the smile beaming across her face. At that moment he was at last convinced that Iowa would be good for another Schoepf family. The following day, Johann led him to meet with Wolfgang Schmidt. Within minutes, David's immediate future was secured.

"You've been talking to your uncle Michael again, haven't you?" boomed John Healy to his eldest child Will. "That's where you got this foolhardy idea, isn't it?" All present at the Healy Sunday dinner table stopped eating when they sensed the family patriarch's deep voice rise. Everyone looked at John, except for Rose, Will's wife, who simply stared down at her plate.

"What does it matter, Father?" Will answered. "Plain and simple, the future I want for my family is not here. As long as we stay, I will be a part-time farmer for you and a part-time blacksmith in town. In the end, I will have nothing to call my own."

"So you think loading up a wife and four children to go off west with no particular destination in mind is a responsible thing to do. How do you plan to put food on the table for six people?" The elder Healy shook his fork as he spoke.

"Thanks to you, Father, I think I have a number of skills. You've taught me well the ways and means of farming, and I've learned blacksmithing from Jared Doolin. I think I can find ways of putting those abilities to good use."

"I still say it was Michael who planted this seed in you."

"And if it was?"

"Then damn him for breaking apart this family." John's voice approached the level of a roar.

"He's not breaking apart anything," replied Will. "He simply enlightened me that there may be more opportunities for me and my family elsewhere. What if he's right? I mean, he's even planning to move his law practice to Fort Dodge this year. He's thinking bigger than Lansing, and that's made me wonder, too. I'm 30 years old and living in a rented house while working two jobs for other men. That's not what I want for my family."

"You're most likely to end up a farmer," John said, "and there's nothing wrong about that. It's paid off for me in northeast Iowa, and it could do so for you as well. And it paid off for Michael, too, until he decided to quit and make a living off the problems of other people. Why not stay and grasp onto a sure thing instead of risking everything for God-knows-what elsewhere?"

"Land is too expensive here, Father. You know that. The days of the $1.25-an-acre farmland are long gone. There's cheaper land in the Dakotas." John Healy simply shook his head and resumed eating his Sunday meal. No one else present dared to start another conversation.

Later, Will's 27-year-old brother Thomas was helping to get Rose and four children into the family buckboard. "Don't let it bother you," Thomas assured him. "He likes to think he knows everything going on around him, and you caught him by surprise. He'll get over it before too long," Thomas reassured him.

"He seems to forget why he left Ireland. And Canada," replied Will.

"I don't think I'd dare to remind him," Thomas said through a smile. He then patted his older brother on the shoulder, turned and walked back toward the house.

Only when Will and his family were nearly a mile out of his father's driveway anyone speak. "I'm proud of you for standing your ground," Rose Healy said to her husband. "I know it can't be easy," she continued. "Your father can be a strong and stubborn man."

"So can I," Will answered. "Maybe that's part of the problem. Sometimes we're too much alike. I just hope that someday he will see that we're doing what we believe is best for us, just like he did in moving from Ireland to Canada and then to Iowa."

"He's not seeing it that way right now. He feels like he's losing a son," Rose said. "Maybe that makes him feel like he failed somehow." For the rest of the ride home, Will pondered quietly. He finally concluded that not only must he be determined to succeed, but he must be equally determined not to fail.

When the first week of May arrived, Will deemed it time for him to pack up his family and start the trip westward. Before leaving, though, he had assisted his father and two brothers in plowing and planting the Healy farmland south of the Wexford Catholic Church. Will noticed in doing so that his father seemed to be at least acclimated to the idea of his moving his family from Allamakee County to somewhere in Dakota Territory. John would occasionally give his son gentle reminders of things he had taught Will years earlier.

"Sharpen your plowshare every evening," John said one afternoon. "It will save wear on your horses. Remember, a man is only as good as his equipment." On those occasions, Will realized the true value of having someone like John Healy for a father.

"Don't worry, Father," Will answered. "You've taught me well. I'll make you proud of me." The elder Healy shrugged and walked away. Will knew that was his father's way of saying "I know."

The planting finished, Will and Rose prepared seven-year-old Albert, five-year-old Edward, three-year-old Mary and toddler Anne, just turned one, for a train trip westward. They knew the tracks had been laid as far west as Sibley, some two hundred miles away. Will was sure that he could find some kind of work there, probably something associated with the building of the Sioux City and St. Paul Railroad. Surely, he reasoned, the railroad would continue to build westward and would need laborers with his skills and work ethic. He was right. Within a day after experiencing the family's first train ride, Will found work as a gandy dancer.

Gandy dancers were part of a 16-man section gang of variously skilled workers who were responsible for laying and maintaining the railroad tracks. Their main job was to put the 400-pound rails in place, starting with situating them on the wooden ties. Then the rails would have to be aligned so that the track would be straight. The section gang used large pry bars and had to work in unison. That necessary teamwork was often achieved using song to keep the men moving in synchronization. The rails would then be leveled, using shims to raise the low spots. Finally, spikes would be driven through holes in the rails to fasten them to the ties below. All of this intense effort was designed to expand the railroad's reach by about a mile a day, depending upon terrain and weather. Will noticed almost immediately that nearly all of the gandy dancers were of Irish descent.

The summer of 1877 was a typically hot one in northern Iowa, making the work of laying track especially strenuous. Each evening, a thoroughly exhausted Will would get off the handcart that he and the rest of his section gang rode to and from the work site. He would arrive at the house that he had rented from the railroad looking forward to nothing more that some peace and rest. Four children had other plans. They swarmed him as he came through the front door. Finally, Rose would serve supper and tuck the children away in bed for the evening, leaving some time for the parents to visit.

Will was lucky, he knew. He had a family to give him reason to work as hard as he did and to keep him doing so. Many of the other railroad workers were unmarried or had left their wives and children somewhere until they could earn enough money to bring them west. Many of them spent most of their hard-earned money on drinking and gambling. Will didn't do that, however, and he knew precisely why.

John Healy raised all of his children, including Will, right. From the stories his father had told him, Will knew that his father had endured his share of hardship in life, from the Potato Famine in Ireland, to a typhoid fever epidemic and discrimination in Canada to a hard life of clearing land to start a farm in Iowa. Will was determined to be the same kind of man as his father, and he had help to do so.

As a teenager in catechism class, Will took note of a girl named Rose Duncan. Rose's family lived a half-mile west of the Wexford church, and her father was a man of integrity, having once served as county treasurer for Allamakee County. In comparison to other girls in the area, Will thought Rose to be rather stern-looking, so it wasn't radiance that caught his attention. Instead, he was fascinated by her lack of a smile. No matter what the occasion, she always appeared dour. For some reason Will himself never understood, he determined to change that.

Every Sunday in church, the Healy family sat in their customary pew directly across from that of the Duncans. Will's first efforts at drawing a smile out of Rose Duncan involved looking intermittently at her throughout the service. After a couple of weeks of futile staring, Will decided he needed a new plan, a plan he didn't have. As it turned out, he didn't need much of one.

On a rainy Sunday morning in June, just after Mass ended, Will saw the Duncans' wagon parked alongside that of the Healys. As Rose and her family were boarding theirs in preparation for the short distance home, Will, a short way away, impulsively broke into a sprint and leaped toward the back of his family's wagon with every intent of landing on his feet on the back of it. Somewhere between leap and landing, however, something must have startled the horses, and the wagon lurched forward a couple of feet. Will landed unceremoniously on his backside on the gravel in the parking lot, tearing his Sunday breeches and coat in the process. At first, Rose gasped in fear that he had hurt himself. Then she broke into laughter and finally the smile Will had been seeking. Assured that he had not seriously hurt himself, she stepped from the Duncan family wagon to comfort him. A lifelong love thus began, punctuated by more of her smiles.

As October crept its way into November, Will Healy faced a problem. The track laying for 1877 was about to shut down for the winter, and most of the gandy dancers would be laid off. The prospect of having no work for several months until the action resumed in the spring weighed on him, and time was running out. Only a limited number of jobs was available in Sibley and Will was not assured of landing one of them. Returning to Lansing was not an option, for a number of reasons. He needed a solution and soon.

"You're a hard worker, Irish," Will heard from behind him as he stopped for a breath after helping to guide a rail into place. "And you don't talk and complain all the time like some of these other louts." Will turned to see who was talking to him. The remark made him edgy. Being called Irish, while true, was not usually a compliment. He turned to see that the comment had come from a man sitting casually on a dun horse, a man William recognized as Charlie, the section foreman of the railroad building crew. The man had a short black beard and piercing dark eyes. Will knew nothing about him beyond his name, though he had heard a few of his colleagues with the Sioux City and St. Paul remark that he was a tough son of a bitch, but a fair one.

"What's more important?" Will asked.

"What do you mean?"

"The worker or the Irish?" Will persisted.

"The worker, of course," was the quick reply. "I personally don't give a damn where a man comes from as long as he lives up to his word. You signed on to give a good day's work in exchange for a fair day's pay. So far as I can see, you've lived up to that. Too bad it's about to end, at least for this year." Will nodded his head in acknowledgement. "Doesn't have to, you know." Will's attention peaked at Charlie's last statement.

"How so?"

"Well, the powers that be, meaning the owners of this railroad company, have decided that we can lay even more track next year if we spend this winter getting ready to do that. They want me to find a crew of about thirty men to do equipment repairs and make rail switches, hand cars and other things we'll need to keep the wheels of progress rolling. Interested?"

"Might be," Will answered, lying only slightly and hoping he didn't seem too enthusiastic. "Tell me more."

"Fifteen dollars for a six-day week. And free housing in a place just up the road."

"Where?"

"Place called Sioux Falls. In Dakota Territory. Kind of a growing town. By the way, ever done any smithing?"

"Yes, I have. Back home."

"Where's that?"

"Lansing. In Allamakee County. I worked for a fellow named Jared Doolin for the past ten years."

"Well, in that case, the wages just went up to eighteen dollars a week, based on your experience. Better say 'yes' pretty soon, Irish. You're costing me more the longer we talk." The smile on the foreman's face sealed the deal for Will.

"Yes."

"Good," was Charlie's reply. "By the way, my name's Charlie Kostboth. And yours?"

"Will. Will Healy." The two men then shook hands.

"I'm from Iowa myself," Charlie said. "McGregor. In Clayton County. And my wife is from Clayton Center."

"I've heard of both of them," Will answered. That evening Will Healy went home as happy as he had been months.

Charlie Kostboth was a man of his word, Will soon discovered. Before a week had passed since their initial conversation, Charlie informed Will that a wagon would come to move Rose, Albert, Edward, Mary and Anne to a wooden house on the south side of Sioux Falls in Dakota Territory. The house had obviously been hastily built by railroad employees, but it had a tar paper covering a wooden exterior, wooden floors and a working stove. While cramped, it could and would easily turn into a home under Rose's touch. The shop where Will was to work was a mere block away. To the Healys, there was no better place or way to spend the winter.

The winter of 1878 passed all too quickly for Will and Rose. Will spent six days each week in a heated shop doing work he knew and liked. With no deadlines pressing him, he could refine the craftsmanship in which he prided himself. He and Rose also spent much of their time socializing with other railroad families, particularly Charlie and his wife Catherina. He learned that Charlie had spent most of the previous three years managing a freight warehouse in McGregor for Joseph "Diamond Joe" Reynolds, who controlled a shipping and railroad empire throughout eastern Iowa. Will guessed that's where Charlie developed his skills at managing a work force. That, and being a born leader.

By late April, after most of the customary spring rains subsided, the Sioux City and St. Paul railroad had started to snake its way westward from Sioux Falls across rolling prairie, pausing occasionally to satisfy its appetite for crushed rock, timber, rails and spikes. The weather throughout the early spring cooperated so much that the mile-a-day goal of the company management was easy to achieve but a difficult pace for suppliers to maintain. In early June, it had reached a place called Marion Junction and stopped. Nearly a full week of steady rain halted progress. When the rain stopped, however, the railroad building did not resume. After two days of no work and no pay, the curious and uneasy workers were called to a mass meeting under a series of huge tents erected as meeting halls. Each section gang was assigned a particular tent. All received the same harsh news. "For economic reasons, the Sioux City and St. Paul Railroad was suspending its expansion operations for the foreseeable future." That meant that all employees were immediately free to leave. The world of the Healy family was rocked hard.

"What will we do?" Rose asked her husband after the children were bedded down for the evening.

"Perhaps what we set out to do," Will answered. "Maybe this is a sign of some kind."

"What do you mean?"

"This may be the place we are meant to be," said Will. "There is a good plenty of cheap, even free, land around here. We've saved enough money to claim some of it and begin farming, even if we don't have much of a crop next year."

"What about this year? asked an obviously concerned Rose. William sat silently for a few moments, rubbing his chin as he thought.

"It's not too late to plant a garden," he finally said. "And we could build a sod house, and I could work the soil to ready it for next year's crops. This may be the chance we left Lansing for, Rose." He tried to sound more excited than afraid. Then he looked silently at his wife. Surprisingly, she smiled back at him.

The following morning, Will Healy went into Sioux Falls and purchased a wagon, two sturdy-looking horses and enough provisions to last what he guessed would last some four months on the prairie. The following day, he presented himself to the land office in a town called Cameron, situated about four miles northeast of where the railroad stopped. While his children waited in the wagon, Will and Rose filed claims on adjoining quarter sections of land about six miles north of Cameron. As they were leaving the land office, they encountered Charlie and Catherina Kostboth, who were on their way in to do the precisely the same thing. Seeing Charlie, whose judgment Will had learned to trust, making the same choice as he assured Will that he was doing the right thing. As he drove the wagon northward from Cameron, Will Healy was sure he was travelling toward a destiny of his own making.

"No!" The word, stated emphatically and loudly, stung the ears and heart of John Schoepf. As he watched the short, sassy Bertha Samp walk boldly from his wagon to her house on a Saturday evening in May, he was stunned into silence. Six months of courtship suddenly seemed wasted.

John and his lookalike brother Matt, a year younger, were considered prime catches among all the bachelors in Elkader. Both were tall, strong but slender and sported sandy blond hair and deep blue eyes. Their neatly trimmed mustaches, well fitting clothes and ready smiles gave them a dashing look that made them the focus of many matrimony-seeking females in the area. John was shocked to find that Bertha Samp was not one of them.

John hoped it was not idea of marriage that Bertha opposed. After all, he knew she had been married before, to an Elkader entrepreneur named Benjamin Buobe, some thirty years her senior. It couldn't have been a marriage of convenience, John reasoned. No children were involved either before or after the vows were spoken in October of 1885. Nor could his appearance, character or reputation in the community be the problem. Even in modesty, he knew of no reason a true-hearted woman would turn his proposal down. Nearly a week would pass before he would find out.

By the following Thursday, John could stand no longer the inexplicable rejection he felt over Bertha Samp's refusal to accept his proposal of marriage. He left early from his job as stable master for the Schmidt brothers' sizable herd of horses kept to serve a multitude of purposes. On the six-mile ride to the village of Elkport where Bertha worked six days a week as a cook at the only local café, he hoped she would still be there when he arrived. All the way to his destination, he rehearsed what he planned to say.

The sun was just starting to dip below the eastern Iowa hilltops when John arrived in Elkport. To his relief, he saw that the café was still open. He tethered his horse and tried to walk confidently into the establishment. As he did, he saw Bertha cleaning up the kitchen. When she in turn saw him, he beckoned her toward the table where he seated himself. Momentarily, she arrived and sat down as he motioned her to do so. Her small dark eyes seemed to bore through him as she waited for him to speak.

"I need to ask you something," John said, getting straight to the point of his presence.

"I've already said 'no'," Bertha said, cutting him off. Still, she made no effort to return to her work. John took that as a good sign.

"I know that," John continued. "But I just want to know why. You know I have some special feelings for you. I've told you that. And you told me you have the same kind of feelings for me. Is that still true?"

"Yes," was Bertha's only response.

"So why will you not agree to marry me?" Difficult as it was, John determined to remain silent until she answered him. Long moments passed before she did.

"I can be a difficult person, John Schoepf. As proof, I offer the fact that I was married before, but that's something I will not talk about. It's in the past, and I will certainly leave it there. That experience taught me some things about what I want if I marry again. And I won't accept less."

"And what is that?" John could feel a ray of hope welling within him, a ray that began to dim as she again looked silently at him. Finally, she spoke.

"You're a good man, John, indeed a splendid one. You have regular employment, you are a joy to look at, and you carry yourself well. You have the best of reputations. All of those things, along with the feelings I know you have for me, are qualities I would like to enjoy for the rest of my life. But you're not your own man, John, and I want someone beholden to no one but me." Once more her eyes pierced him.

"I'm afraid I don't know what you mean."

"You work for others," Bertha replied. "Whether you can support me or any family we raise is dependent upon the whims of others, whether is it the Schmidts or your father. It is so much out of your control, and that frightens me." She was right, John immediately knew. His employment with the Schmidt brothers could end with any unfortunate economic event. Even a mishap in dealing with a horse could cost him his livelihood and put him, Bertha and any family in peril. Also, many of his evenings and weekends were devoted to helping his father and brothers on the farm that his father had finally managed to purchase sixteen years after arriving in Iowa from Germany in 1868. His absence from those duties would create some sort of hardship on David, Matt and young Charley. Maybe Bertha was right, he noted. He really wasn't truly independent.

"Is there anything I can say to change your mind?" John asked, fearful of the answer.

"No," Bertha answered. "But I'm willing to wait awhile for you to do whatever you have to do," she added, with a smile to punctuate it. She then rose and strode confidently to the kitchen to finish her duties for the day. John walked out the door, mounted his horse and rode north toward and beyond Elkader. Three weeks later, he boarded a train westward with no particular destination in mind.

In only a couple of hours' time in the passenger car on the train, John realized that he was blessed to have been raised in the most scenic part of Iowa. After leaving the Mississippi River bluff country behind, he saw nothing but flat farmland and more flat farmland. Only such sizable towns as Nashua, Charles City, Mason City, Algona and Spencer broke up the monotonous view. The ride left John hours to replay three weeks of thoughts.

Bertha was right, he knew. Even though he was earning a fair living tending the Schmidts' horses, he would never truly be economically comfortable. And his employment, though somewhat secure, would never be guaranteed, despite the special talent he had demonstrated for recognizing food horseflesh. Too many factors had to remain in place for that to happen, and those factors were out of his control.

John also knew that the 100-acre David Schoepf farm in Boardman Township did not hold his future, either. At 56, his father was still in good health and energetic enough to manage the farm and reap most of its profits. Neither John nor Matt could earn enough from it to make a living, and only one of them stood to inherit it at some point in the future. John convinced himself that he would do well to step aside for Matt. At 26, John felt the time was ripe to make his own future and that somewhere west, perhaps the newly formed state of South Dakota was the place to go.

Three days after departing Elkader, John stepped off the train in Mitchell, South Dakota, a place he had heard from a fellow passenger contained a land office. That same passenger claimed to have heard that several settlers who had filed homestead claims in the area were selling out, having been scared off by losing much of what they had in a blizzard in January of the previous year. The possibility of acquiring some cheap land to farm, especially if some of the preparation work was already done, appealed to John.

The next day, John caught a train to Spencer, South Dakota, about twenty miles east of Mitchell. What he found when he got there was just what one might expect of a town barely two years old. Some of the original wooden buildings were in the process of replaced by structures made of quartz from a quarry a half-mile south of town. A bank and a school were readily apparent. Commercial activity was obvious everywhere. The buzz of success was in the air.

After only a couple of hours of inquiry, John found a man named A.C. Goltz who owned a 160-acre plot of land that he wished to sell. The farm lay three miles due north of town and had a wooden shack built on it. The land was already plowed and planted, and Goltz was in a hurry to sell so he could return to Ohio and work the family farm he had just inherited from his father. The $7.50 an acre asking price seemed reasonable to John, so by nightfall, he was a no longer an Iowa laborer. Instead he was a South Dakota farmer. Hoping Bertha Samp would be sufficiently impressed with his initiative and potential, he wrote her a letter detailing his accomplishments and told her he would be back to Elkader to claim her as soon as the fall harvest was completed. She wrote him in return that she would indeed be expecting him.

True to his word, John Schoepf returned to Elkader in late fall. On Christmas day, in the presence of Bertha's family, including her parents and nine siblings, he proposed marriage to her. This time, she said "Yes" and with noticeable enthusiasm. They set a date of February 14, 1890, so they could return to South Dakota in time for spring planting. As they hastily planned their wedding, John boasted to his family and friends that the wedding of John Schoepf and Bertha Samp would be the biggest news event of the year in Elkader. He was wrong.

In January of 1890, all of Clayton County was consumed by the progress of the trial of 12-year-old John Wesley Elkins, charged with killing his father and stepmother on the family farm four miles southeast of Littleport the previous July. Elkins initially claimed that an unknown man had entered the house shortly after midnight and committed the crime. By August 1 of 1889, young Elkins confessed that it he himself had performed the heinous deed. He was subsequently sentenced to life imprisonment. Thus were the nuptials of Bertha Samp and John Schoepf upstaged. In mid-February, the newlyweds left Elkader for the final time. A future awaited them, and they were ready to build it. On February 14, John celebrated the occasion by carrying Bertha across the threshold of their shanty in South Dakota.

From the beginning, Bertha Samp Schoepf insisted on being involved in every aspect of running the farm. Not only did she do a good share of the labor, but she demanded that John explain to her the reasoning behind every decision. She also made her voice heard in the process of making those decisions as well. At times, John was reminded of the moment when she stated that she was sometimes a difficult woman. Strong was a better word, he concluded. That sounded much better than difficult.

Building a farm from nearly virgin prairie proved to be labor-intensive for John and Bertha Schoepf. Corn seed needed to be purchased, soil tilled, and crops cultivated periodically until the fall harvest. Dairy cows required daily feeding and watering and twice daily milking. The chickens demanded attention as well. Without complaint, Bertha simply stepped in to do whatever needed to be done, and her husband beamed proudly as she did. Her work ethic likely started as a young girl in Germany, John figured. She told him that she and her nine siblings worked as gleaners, walking through harvested fields to retrieve whatever small bits of product remained. Many times, what they gathered was the meal of the day for the Samp family.

Despite being busy managing his farm in the present, John Schoepf found time occasionally to look to the future. Next year, he thought, he would have the Simmons brothers, a local family of carpenters, build a proper farmhouse large enough to accommodate the family he and Bertha hoped to have. More immediately, he entertained the idea of raising some hogs to use as a source of cash on a regular basis between harvests. He could buy some sows and a boar or two and use them to build up a herd. It seemed to be a good idea, but he knew that his wife should be a part of that decision. One late April evening, he broached the subject with Bertha.

"So you want to raise some pigs, is that it?" she asked as they walked from the field back to their small, simple wooden house.

"Yes," was John's simple response as they continued trudging toward the house.

"Why?

"We could use the company," John joked, smiling at Bertha as he spoke.

"Be careful what wish for," Bertha replied, staring straight ahead as she did.

"Why is that?" queried, totally unsure of her meaning.

"We'll have some sooner than you think." With that remark, she gave him the biggest smile he had seen since their wedding day. He needed a moment to process her message, however. Finally, he composed himself.

"You mean...?" was the best he could offer.

"Yes."

"When?"

"Probably sometime around Christmas, I think." Without awaiting another word of conversation, John Schoepf picked up his wife and carried her the remaining quarter mile home.

On December 23, 1890, Anna Schoepf was born to John and Bertha. Otto followed two years later, then William in 1895. Obviously, John and Bertha Schoepf were raising more than corn, wheat and assorted livestock.

Through the windows of the bedrooms on the second story of his square farmhouse, Will Healy could, by design, survey nearly every one of the 320 acres of the farm he and his wife Rose had established. Using rights provided them under the Homestead Act of 1862, they had each laid claim to 160-acre adjacent quarter sections of flat South Dakota farmland. Will had purposely located the house on the north end of their joint properties so that no long driveway requiring maintenance would be needed. He also saw that the house was in the northeast corner of the quarter-section claimed in his name.

That Healy farmland had been good to them in the nearly twenty years they had worked it. The yields were not as large as those in neighboring Iowa but corn and some wheat crops provided ample profits. Two or three dairy cows, along with some chickens and a handful of hogs at any given time, met the needs of the Healy family, and a growing one it was. Will Healy knew, though, that his success was due to more than good fortune.

After only a few years of farming, Will discovered that he thoroughly loved being a farmer. At first, he saw it as merely a labor-intensive means of supporting himself and his family. Soon, he found that he truly enjoyed the challenges incumbent to producing annual crops on a profitable basis, caring for a small cadre of animals and maintaining equipment in efficient operating condition. He saw the farmer's life as a perpetual series of tests of his will and problem-solving skills, and he was happy to note that he passed more of them than he failed.

"You're a very good planner," Rose had once told Will. "That's one of the things I most admire about you." She had spoken those reassuring words just before they had left Allamakee County in 1877. He needed to hear them then, to ease the self-doubt he had at the time. Those words served him well then and on many occasions since. Every winter, Will devoted time to plan his work for the following year.

Corn and wheat were the staple cash producers on the Healy farm. Those crops consumed 160 growing acres of land each year. Another 100-acre tract was left fallow on a rotating basis. Will believed that land could be worn out by continuous hosting of the same crop year after year and that rotating the use of each parcel of land could give nature a chance to replenish the topsoil's nutrients. Leaving each field completely untilled every third year served to hasten that process. Some of his neighbors thought it foolish to have unproductive land. "It's just lost money," they sometimes said. Will said nothing and allowed his land to generate better crop yields year after year.

The forty acres of the Healy farm adjacent to the barn were designated as hay land and annually produced enough hay to feed the small herd of Holsteins through the year, including the winter months. That particular location made storing the hay in the barn a relatively easy task, for the hay needn't be moved far. Will wanted no part of beef cattle, though. He had seen what happened to sizable herds of beef cattle during terrible blizzards in 1880 and again in 1888. Far too many of his friends and neighbors had been financially ruined on those occasions, and he determined that that would not happen to his farm. The remaining ten acres or so hosted the house, barn, hog house, chicken coop and a shelter belt William planted in the spring of 1880. In simple terms, Will knew that the cows, hogs and chickens fed the family. Corn and wheat kept them housed, clothed and working.

Will and Rose Healy had left Iowa with four children in tow. Agnes joined the group in 1878, followed by Esther in 1881, William Jr. in 1883, Theresa in 1886, Katherine in 1888, James in 1890 and finally Rosalie in 1894. With a loving wife, a large stable family and a solid farming operation in his grasp, Will felt, that at 51 years old, he had endured many tests life presented him and managed to survive and thrive. He looked forward to many more years of prosperity and contentment. Then he could leave a legacy of well-raised children and well tended land. As he had promised his father twenty years ago, he would make the elder Healy proud. Shortly before his death in 1894, John had told his oldest son as much. Will valued that acknowledgement as much as anything in his life.

The first Saturday of every month was normally go-to-town day for the entire Healy clan. When morning chores were done, each family member washed and awaited Will's command to load the wagon for the five-and-a-half mile ride to the bustling town of Canistota. Once there, Will and Rose would purchase whatever supplies the farm did not provide, such as fabric Rose would magically transform into clothing. She loved to sew, Will knew. Soon, he determined, he would have to buy her a sewing machine. The trip to Canistota also gave all the Healys a chance to socialize and catch up on local news. The first Saturday in July was no different. For the children, the promise of a stick or two of hard candy hastened their preparations for the day.

"You're still a good worker, Irish," Will heard while he loaded some flour and sugar into the wagon, careful to keep it out of the way of passengers on the return journey. He paused his efforts to turn and address his friend Charlie Kostboth.

"But I'm still Irish," Will replied, "and proud of it." He flashed Charlie another of the quick smiles the two had exchanged since working together on the Sioux City and St. Paul Railroad in 1877 and 1878.

"Well, we all have our faults," Charlie quipped. "I forgive that you were born with yours and that can't be helped."

"That should cost you lunch."

"Agreed." With that, the two men walked across the street to the local café. Once there, they found their wives with the same plan. The four of them sat together.

"I've been meaning to talk to you about something, Will," Charlie said as their table was being cleared and their coffee cups refilled. "Seeing you here today saves me a ride to your place."

"And what is that?" asked Will.

"As long as I've known you, you've been an honest man unafraid to speak your mind. And you have obviously made a success of your farm and family. Have you ever thought about running for public office?" Charlie waited for Will to make the next remark. It came quickly.

"No, absolutely not." Will knew that Charlie had served in the state legislature in 1893 and 1894, and he didn't know how a man with eight children and a farm to maintain could find the time to do justice to a job in Pierre, the state capitol, nearly two hundred miles away. He admired Charlie for having done so, but he wanted no part of it himself. Besides, he had no taste for politics. "Anyway, I probably couldn't win anyway. This is a Republican state, and I tend to be a Democrat on most matters."

"All the more reason to do it," argued his friend. "Someone has to present the other side of issues, don't they? Isn't that how government is supposed to work? And I think I can help you get elected. After all, I'm a Republican, and if I speak up on your behalf, people will listen. I think you should give it some thought. You know as well as I that you could let your sons run your farm while you're away. They're more than capable. They've had good teaching. The House of Representatives needs you, Will. The 11th District seat is up for election next year, and I'd like to see you fill it."

"What makes you think I could do it?"

"You're president of the school board for Cameron #110, aren't you? You must have some idea about how the process works, I would think." Charlie was referring to the country school a half-mile west of the Healy farm.

"That's only because most of the kids in that school are mine. And I don't have to go two hundred miles away to do the job."

"Look," Charlie said. "Will you promise me that you'll at least give it some serious thought?"

"I guess I could do that," Will said reluctantly.

The ride north toward home was silent for the first half until Rose broke the silence. "Are you going to do it?" she asked.

"You mean run for office, or think about it?" a pensive Will replied.

"Run for office," was her smiling response. "You'd be very good as a representative."

"What makes you think so?"

"Well, let's see. You're smart, successful, hard-working. And honest. We can't forget that," she added.

"That last one should just about rule me out, shouldn't it?" Will smiled as he uttered that last sentence.

"Why, William Healy," Rose exclaimed in obviously fake indignation. "Legislators aren't all dishonest. Look at Charlie, for example. Surely you don't think he is dishonest, do you?"

"No, Charlie's the exception. He told me as much. That's part of the reason he didn't run for re-election. That, and he didn't want to spend any more time away from home."

"The boys and I can manage the farm," Rose answered. "Don't let that hold you back. Besides, it would be in the winter, wouldn't it? You wouldn't be missing as much as you would during any other time of the year." She was right, Will knew, but he also knew he didn't have the passion for the subject that his friend did, and that could be a problem.

"What would you have me do?" Will asked Rose.

"For now, I just want you to think about it. All these years, you've devoted yourself to making me and the children provided for and happy. I think it's about time you did something that you want to do for yourself. You've earned that, William Healy. Just promise me you'll give it some serious thought." Will's only acknowledgement was a smile toward his wife.

The following day was Sunday, and that meant the Healys would make another journey, one they all made every week except during the harsh grip of winter. Canistota had no Catholic church, so the family would again load up into the wagon and travel six miles northeast to St.Patrick's Catholic Church in Montrose.

When railroads were granted parcels of free land to use as a right-of-way for their tracks, there were also given land to sell in order to finance their huge undertakings. Some of that railroad land was to be designated for exclusive use as schools like the one the Healy children attended. Other plots of land, roughly ten or so miles apart, were to be set aside for the establishment of towns where trains could stop and take on water and firewood and in which people could eventually settle. Travelers venturing west from Sioux Falls would find themselves in hastily constructed villages such as Hartford, Humboldt, Montrose, Salem and Spencer, to name a few. By 1897, each of those communities was a thriving commercial center.

From the beginning in 1880, the population of Montrose was mostly Irish, and for no particular reason. It was a typical self-contained community with the usual array of grain elevator, grocery stores, cafes, farm implement dealers, a blacksmith shop, a couple of doctors and a bank. All of those enterprises were prepared to capitalize on the infant farming economy in northeastern McCook County. The town also had a Methodist church, a Presbyterian church and St. Patrick's Church. The latter drew the Healys to the town. The dominant Irish population gave them more of a communal feeling than they found in Canistota.

The Mass this particular Sunday was the usual long one, made somewhat uncomfortable by the omnipresent July heat. Will spent much time watching Rose try to keep seven-year-old James from entertaining himself by pestering older sisters Teresa and Katherine. The boy had enough energy to continually get into trouble and a charming, eye-twinkling smile to get him out of it. He was a rare source of irritation, charm and pride, all at the same time.

Father Ryan's homily for the week dealt with the subject of serving one's fellow man and the need to seek out ways to do so. "Don't wait for such opportunities to present themselves to you," the priest implored. "Seek them out, and you shall be rewarded with as much joy as you give." Those ideas stuck in Will's mind and rolled in his thoughts on the wagon ride home.

When the Healys returned home shortly after noon, Rose ushered the girls into the house to prepare the customary Sunday family dinner. Will, accompanied by James, went to the barn to unhitch the horses and feed them. As he did so, he looked out the west door of the barn at the hayfield. Tomorrow would be a good day to start the second cutting of the season, he noted. The unusually dry summer had delayed that event by about two weeks, but the hay was finally ready. William hoped he could get a third cutting in before wheat and corn harvest began.

Early in their marriage, Will and Rose Healy determined that unless necessary reason existed, Sundays were to be celebrated in the Biblical sense. Only such duties as feeding animals and milking cows were performed, but no others. Hence, everyone got an opportunity to enjoy some personal time. Rose enjoyed sewing and spent much of the afternoon and evening repairing and making clothing for the children. Will generally used the time to plan his work for the week ahead. They both knew they were not literally following the idea of the Sabbath, but rationalized to each other that as long as they were doing what they liked, they were breaking no rules. Only planting season and the fall harvest changed that routine.

Monday morning broke hot and dry, as each day of the previous month had done. Nevertheless, there was work to be done, and Mother Nature didn't seem to care about the comfort of those who had to do it. After the cows were milked and breakfast eaten, Will, along with Edward, William Jr. and an eager James went through the barn to begin the tedious process of cutting and transporting hay from the acreage west of the barn to and into the structure. Will would do the cutting, William Jr. would load it onto a horse-drawn sled and, when full, guide it to the barn, where he would help Edward unload it onto a platform and use a pulley to lift it to the loft. Once there, the two older sons would unload it into its second-story home, to be stored until needed. Meanwhile, young James would help his father by gathering the hay into piles for his older brothers to process. The youngest Healy boy seemed to enjoy his duties. His father guessed that that was because it provided him with two things he valued, activity and a feeling of importance.

The entire process of cutting and storing hay usually required four days of the same procedure followed countless times. Laborious as it was, though, the Healy boys knew it was essential to the success of their farm. Cows needed to eat, and some of the hay could be sold to farmers who raised herds of feeder cattle. In a dry year like 1897, a tidy sum could result. The effort would be rewarded in one, if not two, ways.

As he stopped for a moment to catch his breath, Will Healy saw his son James drop an armful of hay and run off in the direction of a rabbit he had apparently scared up in his hay cutting. As he raised his hand and started to speak to his son, Will felt a sharp pain in the left side of his chest. No words came from his mouth. Slowly he sank to a kneeling position. The last thing he saw was William Jr. running toward him, mouth agape and eyes wide open.

1906

Faith, tradition and family, in that order, ruled Bertha Schoepf's life. As a lifelong practicing Lutheran, she saw that her family made the three-mile trip southward to Spencer each Sunday for worship services. Even the worst of a prairie winter seldom kept John, Bertha and their six children from devoting a portion of their lives to God. Bertha truly believed that her family would be rewarded for the good life they lived.

Tradition filled in where faith was vague. Bertha believed that there were certain things in life that needed doing at certain times just because that was the case. One such thing happened every year at the first of the year. It was then that she sat at her kitchen table for hours composing a letter to her parents, August and Augusta Samp of Elkader, Iowa. Writing that letter was something she had done faithfully every year since she and John had arrived in South Dakota in 1890. Each year's edition was first and foremost, an update of the previous year in the lives of the South Dakota Schoepfs. In 1899, 1901 and 1903, the main news was the birth of yet another son, George, John Jr. and Reinhnold, respectively.

The annual state-of-the-farm report was also a constant part of Bertha's letter. Some years, like 1895, 1898, 1901 and 1904, were good ones. 1894, 1900 and 1905, however, were dry years and, thus, not so prosperous. Every year, however, yielded at least enough crops to pay the taxes and bills and leave at least a little left over. Some of each year's surplus was used for home improvements. As far as Bertha was concerned, farming in South Dakota was a good life.

On January 1, 1906, Bertha sat at her table, pen, paper and ink bottle before her, searching for a cheerful way to begin her annual letter. 1905 had been perhaps the most difficult of years for Bertha and her family, but she didn't want to sound depressed. She had too much pride for that, and she knew that, despite being nearly forty years old, her parents still considered her their daughter and would capitalize on any reason to worry about her well-being. Besides, the Schoepfs had endured difficult years in the past and would likely see prosperous ones in the future.

Jan. 1, 1906

Dearest Mother and Papa,

I hope this letter finds you and the rest of the family in Iowa to be well. I think of you often, especially during these long winter months.

Your grandchildren are all doing well. Anna is now just turned fifteen years old and has begun to attract notice from boys, especially a young man named Wilbur Matkins, who comes from a fine family of solid standing. Otto and William have taken on a good many of the responsibilities of keeping the farm working. They are both hard workers and seem to enjoy what they do. I feel badly, though that they have stopped attending school in order to be of help at home. George is a typical boy who likes to follow his older brothers about and do whatever they do, whether he is capable or not. During the warm weather months, he can usually be found hunting rabbits and squirrels or lying about the shore of Lake Ely waiting for fish to bite.

John Jr. turned four this past April. On Saturday last, I took him to town with me to buy some supplies. As soon as we reached the general store, he climbed down from the wagon on his own and began to wander among the horses and wagons parked on Main St. When I finally caught up to him, he was standing next a horse, petting its leg. Before I could pick him up and remove him from danger, he looked at me and smiled. "Horses, Momma. Horses", he said. "Just like his father", I thought. I often told John that if he ever ran off and left me, it would be for a horse and not another woman. Reinhold just turned two and seems to be doing well.

As for John, he developed a cough in the spring and has been unable to stop it. He has lost a noticeable amount of weight which he didn't have to spare. Also, he can't do much labor without becoming short-winded and coughing, sometimes with bloody results. He continues to make the effort, however, and I do so admire him for that. Dr. Tilley said it is most likely due to consumption. We've seldom talked about where that may lead, and, as for myself, I try not to think about the likely outcome. Instead, I pray for the best.

Last year was a difficult one for farming. Rain was scarce and wind blew constantly. Our corn crop averaged only 35 bushels an acre, about ten less than a normal year. Fortunately we raised some cattle and hogs to help us get by. We have every reason to believe that 1906 will be a better year. We have not had two bad years in a row since settling here sixteen years ago.

Until next year, love to all of you.

Your dutiful daughter, Bertha

During January and February of 1906, more snow blanketed the eastern South Dakota prairie than Bertha could recall seeing in sixteen years of living there. Only a small portion of it came via the violent blizzards she had known since 1891. Most of it came by way of steadily falling snowflakes at a rate of an inch or two each week.

That was good, Bertha knew, for it meant that the toll taken upon the Schoepf farmland from the dry winds of 1905 was being replenished by the winter of 1906. The soil would once again be ready to produce a bounty.

When March gave way to April, the snow gave way to rain, the slow steady kind that soaked into the ground and not the kind that fell harshly and washed away soil as it arrived. That gave Bertha more reason to be encouraged about the coming months, but it wasn't the only one. As the weather warmed, her husband John's coughing spells seemed to abate. They happened only a handful of times each day. Perhaps Doc Tilley was wrong, Bertha mused. Maybe John was on the road to recovery.

Even though John lacked the stamina to do much of the spring planting, he was patient and even cheerful in teaching Otto and William the techniques of hitching the horses to the plow and guiding it through the soft soil to prepare It for the year's seed. Bertha noticed that Otto took to the task in all seriousness, an ever-present look of grim determination on his face. William was much more lighthearted about the job. No crooked furrow would ruin his day. He would simply shrug it off and re-plow it, much to his father's frustration.

"You're wasting horsepower again, son!" Bertha heard her husband shout to William as the boy seemed to wander aimlessly through the field. "The idea is to plow the field once, not twice." William would pretend not to hear him, and, eventually, John would excuse himself to the house. On more than one occasion, he told Bertha that watching their second son do something was much more exhausting than doing it himself. Such a scene typified the big difference between the two boys. Otto was the serious task-focused one, ever eager to live up to responsibilities. William was a charmer, quick with a smile that would immediately disarm anyone at the peak of frustration with him.

Throughout planting season, John was constantly shadowed by his son John, Jr. John knew that it wasn't his own charms that drew young John close to him every time the father went outside the house. No, he realized that he and his son shared a passion for horseflesh.

Before leaving Elkader, Iowa, in 1890, John had been the stable manager for the Schmidt Brothers, a family with many and varied business interests throughout Clayton County and beyond. After only a short time on the job, he realized that he didn't just do the job; he had a passion for horses. They might be his true calling, he concluded. That feeling had not changed after moving to Spencer. On many a Saturday afternoon, when the Schoepf family went to town to shop and socialize, John would walk to Lindekugel's Livery to look over the horses for sale. On rare occasion, he would buy or trade for one or two, but, generally, he just liked the looking. When he did deal, he knew that there was a reason a horse would be for sale, and he prided himself on finding it. If he were to buy someone else's problem, he wanted to know what that problem was. Only then would he know whether or not he wanted to deal with it. Now it seemed his namesake son had inherited his interest.

Each day throughout the spring, John tended to the two pair of draft horses which were the lifeblood of the family farm. As he did so, he explained in detail to his tag-along just what he was doing and why. He knew his son wasn't absorbing everything he was being told and shown. But he believed repetition would eventually solidify the messages. Also, he admired the boy's absolute fearlessness among creatures up to thirty times his weight. The animals responded positively to him, too. Despite his physical limitations, John considered 1906 to be his most enjoyable spring in years. His wife saw that he was happier than he had been for at least two years.

By late May, the corn and wheat crops were planted, and the first cut of haying began. At that time, John's coughing spells became more numerous and intense. Thinking that dust in the air from handling hay in the barn was the primary culprit, he excused himself from all outdoor activities and confined himself to the house until the haying was finished. When the coughing persisted through June and yielded more and more blood, his mood darkened.

"We need to talk, John," Bertha said one late night after the children had settled for the night. John just sat silently staring out the window at the farm he had helped build. "We both know your condition is not getting better," she continued. "We need to do something to change that."

"And what would that be?" John asked without redirecting his gaze toward her.

"You heard Doc Tilley last week," Bertha pressed. "He said that a change of location might help. Someplace like the hospital in Hot Springs."

"We have no money for that," John snapped.

"Then maybe the state hospital in Yankton." Bertha sat silent awaiting a response. She knew what the next statement would be, but she didn't want to be the one to make it.

"If I go anywhere, I don't expect to return, except in a box." John finally said. For the only time ever, Bertha lied to her husband.

"John Schoepf" Bertha barked. "You can't think like that. You're going to get better. We have to put our trust in God to make you right." No more needed to be said. Bertha saw tears welling in her normally stoic husband's eyes. Shortly they began to flow freely. She raced across the room to console him. The more he sobbed, the closer she held him.

June was a wet month, good for farming but not for John Schoepf. The chronically humid air intensified his coughing spasms. By the end of the month, his ribs were always painful and constant headaches became a part of his daily life. Bertha noticed that he was often silent and distant in his thoughts and short-tempered with his children. They, in turn, learned to shy away from him, not knowing what, if any response he would make. He was also uncommunicative with his wife. By the second week of July, Bertha had enough of waiting for her faith to resolve the matter. She took the matter into her own hands. She waited until bed time and slid over to him. His back was toward her, as had become his custom of late. She moved close to his ear and softly said, "I think it's time, don't you?" His reply was barely audible but short and unmistakable in meaning.

"Yes," was all he said.

The sun rose the following morning to find Bertha Schoepf packing a large suitcase of clothing and personal items for her husband to take for his stay at the state hospital in Yankton, some 70 miles away. She knew she should be packing two suitcases, but she told herself that John would only be away for a short time, then would be back home with his family, an idea she was still trying to believe herself.

Bertha helped Anna, her oldest, prepare and serve breakfast for the other five children. Neither parent had much of an appetite at the moment. Shortly before 8:00 a.m., Otto had a team hitched to the wagon, and Bertha and John left for Spencer to catch a train for Salem, ten miles east. From there, trains left for the southward trip to Yankton every two hours on the odds. The entire round trip required no more than six hours, so Bertha planned to be home easily before sundown. That gave her most of a full day to figure out how to explain to her children what was happening. She hoped her faith would help her do that.

Later that evening, Bertha gathered her family around the dining room table to explain the situation regarding their father. "You all know Papa has been sick for awhile," she started. "And he has been trying and waiting to get better. Well, nothing anyone has been able to do, including Doc Tillley, has worked. So, Doc Tilley said we should send him to the hospital in Yankton where he can get more doctoring until he gets well." She looked intently at each child, one by one.

"Isn't that the place for lunatics and insane people?" Anna asked.

"There are all kinds of patients there," Bertha a reassured her. "And he is close enough to home that we can go see him sometimes until he's better."

"Why is Papa sick?" inquired John Jr.

"I don't know," his mother said. "Sometimes it's just God's way." As Bertha looked at him, she saw his fists clench and his face contort into a pained look.

"Then I don't like God! He's hurting my Papa!" He then stormed off toward his bedroom. Bertha knew she would have to provide him with comfort but that the present moment was not the time for that.

Throughout the rest of July and the whole of August, Bertha and her family immersed themselves into the family farming operation. Almost every evening, she would discuss with Anna, Otto and William, the oldest ones, what needed to be done the next day. Then she would step in wherever needed, using the knowledge of farming that learned from her distant husband.

Over this time, Bertha watched Anna develop mothering skills with her three youngest brothers, George, John and Reinhold. All the while that happened, Otto dedicated himself more than usual to doing what needed doing. Surprisingly, even William became more focused on completing tasks on time and in a quality manner. Clearly, Bertha thought, if there was any blessing in their current situation, it was the fact that the Schoepfs had responded in true family fashion. That's something of which she and her husband could be proud.

On three Saturdays, Bertha packed up her family and made the trip to Yankton to see John. Each of the visits followed the same agenda. The presence of his family obviously boosted John's spirits. He spent time asking each individual what they had been doing recently and was genuinely interested in their responses. Bertha involved herself in each conversation, to reaffirm the details of each child's recent life and to keep the exchanges from turning negative. Finally, it was Bertha's turn. Each time she could see fatigue in his eyes and hoped he didn't see the sadness in hers. She knew the visit was about to end and was afraid there wouldn't be another. Finally, a tear-laden departure marked the time for an almost silent return to Spencer.

August 29, 1906, was a typically hot summer day in southern South Dakota. Leaves had begun to brown at the edges in anticipation of their annual chameleon-like demise. On that day, John Carl Schoepf died painfully of tuberculosis in the South Dakota State Hospital in Yankton, South Dakota.

John Schoepf's funeral in Spencer was well-attended. As a sixteen-year resident of a predominantly German Lutheran community, he was member in good standing. That status alone ensured a strong turnout. John's father, David, an Elkader, Iowa, farmer, was present, along with John's siblings, Mattias of Forest City, Iowa, Anna Heiden and Charley, all of Elkader. John's mother Margarethe had passed away due to stomach cancer in 1901.

"If there is anything I can do to help, please let me know," Bertha heard as a hand was placed on her shoulder. She turned to see that the speaker was John's brother Mattias, a year younger than John and nearly a look-alike. "I've been there, believe me." Bertha knew he was right. In 1900, his wife Hanna had suddenly died, leaving him to raise three children aged two, four and five.

"I know" she whispered. "I know." She placed her hand on his and left it there for a moment for emphasis.

Long after all others had left the graveside, John Jr. was reluctantly carried away by Anna and Otto.

1918

The short, thin woman with a baby thoroughly wrapped and held tightly against her was supremely happy to open the door to Haney's Market on South Broadway Avenue in Minot, North Dakota, on a harsh winter day in January of 1918. The two-block walk against a west wind was brutal, and she found herself wishing she had made the trip a couple of days earlier when the wind was not blowing so strongly. Even waiting until early afternoon had not helped much. A heated store full of shoppers offered welcome warmth just when she needed it most.

Even though the woman knew precisely what she intended to buy, she diligently walked the length of each of the eight aisles in the store. She tried to be casual so as to enjoy the indoor climate, but she couldn't quite accomplish that. Her tension was soon validated. Two gunshots broke the frigid air, followed by the tinkling of shattered glass hitting the floor of the market. After some shrieking and ducking for cover by those inside, silence reigned. Momentarily, the owner, Jacob Haney assured those present that it was safe to get up. The woman with the baby scurried to the front counter to pay for her purchases and hastened out the door toward the shotgun-style railroad house she and her husband rented. The punishing wind was fortunately at her back as she went.

Upon entering the house, the woman made sure the baby was calm. She then tucked the infant into his bed, covered him and stood watching until the child fell fast asleep. She was relieved that what they had endured happened so close to the child's naptime. She then heaved a sigh of relief and sat in a chair. She knew that she and her baby had been lucky, but she was terrified that their good fortune would run out at any unannounced moment. After all, they lived in Minot.

In many ways, Minot, North Dakota was a typical railroad town, one of many that sprang up as a result of James J. Hill's Great Northern Railway. Though first platted in 1886 and organized in 1887, it almost immediately took on its nickname of "Magic City", a place where anything and everything goes. Untaxed liquor flowed freely and opium dens occupied any available space. Stolen property moved smoothly through a series of underground tunnels. Although much of that sort of activity happened in what was called the "High Third" area, its unsavory characters managed to spill over into the rest of the city, including downtown. When they did, they took their grudges and criminal behavior with them. As a result, fights, stabbings and shootings were likely to occur at any time and any place. What the woman and her infant had experienced was an all-too-common event in Minot.

When Jim Healy returned from his job overseeing a track maintenance crew for the Great Northern Railway, he had no idea that something was amiss with his wife Mary. She had supper prepared and served him, as usual. She had also set young Joseph at the table and fed him as well. Only when Mary paused midway through clearing the table and tears began to run softly down her cheeks did Jim realize she was distraught. He rose from his chair, walked to her, and put his arms around her to comfort her. "What's wrong, Dear?" he asked. For a few moments there was no answer.

"I don't want to be here anymore," Mary sobbed. Again, there were several minutes of silence between the two.

"What happened?" Jim eventually asked. Mary composed herself just enough to reply.

"J-J-Joey and I w-were in Haney's t-t-today," she stammered uncharacteristically, "and-and there w-w-was shooting, and-and – and a window w-was shot out." She resumed her sobbing into him.

"My God!" Jim exclaimed. "Was anyone hurt?"

"N-no, but we c-could have been." Again she sobbed. "I don't want to stay here anymore, " she finally said. "It's not safe."

"Where do you want to go?" Jim asked.

"Home. Back to South Dakota." Her answer struck him silent.

Despite his outward reaction to his wife's desire to leave Minot, Jim Healy was not surprised to hear it. In fact he had been considering it himself for several weeks. They had left South Dakota for Minot the previous summer after becoming Mr. and Mrs. James Healy. They wanted, as so many do, an opportunity to carve out their own piece of the American dream. That included a prosperous farm and a large family. For that dream to be realized, though, Jim needed a stake. When his cousin John notified him that jobs with good wages were plentiful in North Dakota, he and Mary quickly accepted the task. They, along with their newborn son Joseph, would go to Minot where Jim would earn enough money to save whatever was needed to buy farmland. Good land was cheap there, according to John. A couple of years working for the railroad should enable Jim and Mary to save enough to reach their goal.

Immediately after moving to Minot, the Healys discovered two things that affected their plans. The first was that, unknown to them, even though jobs and money were readily available, the entire city was a seller's market. The prices of everything a young family would need were at least twice what existed in South Dakota.

Saving money would be difficult, they quickly realized. The open-air criminal activity made living expensively a perpetually dangerous venture, as Mary had discovered earlier in the day.

Jim Healy was by far the most extroverted of the ten children of William and Rose Healy. As a boy, he demonstrated a boundless curiosity and a willingness to explore and ask questions of anyone. He also had a natural skill for listening to the responses to his inquiries. Those people skills got him an immediate supervisory assignment with the Great Northern as soon as he arrived in Minot. The word of his cousin, himself a Great Northern employee and man of good repute, didn't hurt, either.

His role with the Great Northern required that Jim supervise a crew of eight men responsible for keeping a twenty-mile stretch of track open and in good repair. The amount of traffic that track received guaranteed that the job would never be finished. There was always wind-deposited debris to clear and regular repairs required. Jim's crew consisted of men who were Irish and somewhat older than he. Despite the age difference they all responded well to his direction. It seemed that he could have as much of a future with the railroad as he wanted. He wondered, though, if that would be enough.

As Jim saw his present situation, leaving Minot was the easiest of the things that lay before him and Mary. The comfortable living arrangement they had left behind in South Dakota no longer existed. When Jim informed his mother Rose that he and Mary wanted to seek their own fortune elsewhere, Rose had sold the east half of the 320-acre Healy farm and made arrangements to rent out the remaining half. In all likelihood, there was little, if any, possibility of returning to his former place in the family business, at least for the current year. That meant the Knewell family hardware store in Dell Rapids, a possibility Jim dreaded.

Despite his demonstrated people skills and natural self-assurance, Jim Healy had been involved in two discussions in his lifetime that he hoped not to repeat. The first occurred when he asked Mary's father for her hand in marriage. It was not an easy sell. Alfred Knewell sternly demanded to know just how his daughter's suitor planned to be a dutiful husband to her and a father to any children they might have. Each question Alfred asked drew a nervous reply, and each reply resulted in tense moments before the next question came forth. After a half-hour of tense drama, Alfred simply stood and proffered his hand to his future son-in-law.

The second stomach-churning conversation of Jim's' life happened when he informed his mother that he and Mary had decided to go to North Dakota, leaving Rose with no means of continuing the farming operation. All nine of Jim's brothers and sisters openly renounced any interest in the business. Hence, he helped his mother arrange the sale of the east 160 acres to Clifton Jacobs and the rental of the remaining half to Oscar Parry. Jim recalled his mother repeatedly questioning the necessity of moving to an unfamiliar place to start a married life and family, and how she became more and more distraught as the conversation continued. Jim reminded her that she and his father Will had done the same thing in moving from northeast Iowa to what was then Dakota Territory forty years earlier, Rose answered that that was a different situation. They had owned no land in Iowa, nor could they afford to. Jim, on the other hand, already managed a successful farm that would eventually be his. Why gamble on North Dakota when South Dakota was a sure thing, she asked her youngest son.

As Jim Healy sat in the living room of his rented home in Minot, he knew that an obvious decision had been reached and only needed to be formalized through verbalization. The idea that he would probably be involved in one, possibly two, humbling conversations loomed inevitable. He would have to admit failure, and that was not a pleasant prospect. The importance of maintaining his personal dignity paled, he knew, in comparison to the safety and happiness of his family. Finally, he broke a long silence.

"Mary?" he queried.

"Yes?" was her simple reply.

"It's time for us to go home."

Mary rose from her chair and walked the three steps to his. She then sat on his lap, and they hugged a long hug.

Three weeks later, the first day of the Healy family trip from Minot to South Dakota ended in Fargo, another thriving commercial hub of the Northern Plains. At first glance, it looked much like Minot, only bigger. A leisurely dinner, restful evening and hot breakfast in a downtown hotel were followed by boarding a train bound for Sioux Falls, South Dakota. The Healys would be departing the train one stop earlier in Dell Rapids, Mary's home town.

Mary's family knew in advance when she, Jim and the infant Joey would be arriving, so Mary's brother Walter was waiting for them at the train station ready to give them a ride to the family house downtown. A room had been prepared for the visitors, Walter said. The reception was genuinely warm, and Jim felt it was sincere.

After breakfast the next morning, Alfred Knewell started the conversation Jim was dreading. Jim could sense it coming when the table was cleared and coffee cups were re-filled. At that point, Alfred took a slow sip of coffee, put the cup down and looked his son-in-law directly in the eyes, which suddenly seemed to Jim to be daggers.

"So what do you plan to do now?" Alfred asked. He continued staring as he awaited an answer.

"I don't know yet, sir," Jim said. "I thought maybe I'd find a job in Sioux Falls for a year or so, then go to Canistota to work my mother's farm."

"I thought she sold that," Alfred commented.

"Only half of it. The other half is rented out, at least for this year. I figure there's a chance I can work that half next year.

"Sounds like a good enough plan," Alfred said, displaying no emotion whatsoever. "I want you to know, though, that I can always use a good man in my business. And you are a good man, son." With that, Alfred lit his pipe and absorbed the latest edition of the local newspaper. He probably had no idea how relieved Jim felt at that moment, or why.

Having been constantly involved in outdoor activity for his entire life, Jim could tolerate only so much indoor confinement, even in the dead of winter. After two days of visiting the Knewells, he was ready to move on, so he, Mary and Joey boarded a train which would eventually take them to Montrose. From there, they would rent a horse and buggy for the six-mile trip to the Healy farm, where Rose was expecting them. Again they were greeted warmly and offered living space for as long as they wanted to stay. Again, as expected, the same potentially ugly conversation Jim hoped to avoid arose, albeit a little less nerve-wracking with his mother than he expected with his father-in-law.

"So what now?" Rose asked her son as she was preparing supper, assisted by Mary.

"I wish I could undo what I've done," Jim replied. "I wish I could buy back the 160 acres you sold and cancel the rental agreement with Oscar Parry. Then we'd have our farm back, and I could build it back up to what it used to be."

"Is that what you want? Really?" Rose asked.

"Yes, I think so," her son said.

"So why don't you try?"

"It's a little late, don't you think? I mean, don't farmers already have their plans made for this year?"

"Where's the harm in asking?"

Before he could think of an answer, Jim realized she was right. He determined that his mission the very next day would be to find and approach Clifton Jacobs and Oscar Parry to see if any business could be done with them.

Clifton Jacobs was easy to find. He was tending to a pen of hogs at his home place just two miles away from the Healy farm on the road to Canistota. His reaction to Jim's proposal to buy the land that Rose sold him a year earlier was brusque and unmistakable in meaning.

"No!" he said, waving a weathered hand as he did. Jim noted that Jacobs was barely thirty years old. He knew that Clifton was unmarried and a relatively newcomer to the area. Hence, not only was the chance of buying the lost acres non-existent for the moment, but didn't look good in the foreseeable future, either. Jim ventured forth toward town.

The noon whistle blew in Canistota that day, and Jim hoped he would find Oscar Parry in the local café for lunch. He was right. Parry, Jim remembered, was a burly man with a full beard. His wife had died suddenly four years earlier, leaving him with a son to raise. Oscar had a deep voice and a hearty laugh that he was quick to use. Parry was sitting alone for the moment, so Jim took advantage of the opportunity to make the large man his captive audience.

"Mr. Parry?" James said. "I don't know if you remember me or not, but I'm Jim Healy, and I have some business I'd like to discuss with you."

"Sure, I remember you, boy" Parry bellowed. "You're Rose Healy's son. The one from North Dakota."

"Not anymore. I've come back."

"It's good to see you, boy, but just what kind of business could we have to discuss?"

Somewhat hesitantly, Jim forged on. "I'm wondering if you are still planning to rent my mother's land this year."

"I plan to." After a swig of coffee, he looked directly at James. "Is that why you came back, to take over the farm?" James simply nodded. "Well, I guess you'll have to wait a year for that to happen." Sensing defeat, Jim started to rise from his seat. "Not so fast, young fellow," Parry said. Quickly, Jim sat down. "We may be able to come to some kind of arrangement." Again, Parry swilled coffee.

"Such as..." Jim pushed the conversation forward.

"As it happens, my son Francis, seems excited about the United States getting into the war going on in Europe. Claims it's his duty to get involved. So excited that he's gone and enlisted in the army. Personally, I don't like the idea. I mean, what goes on halfway across the world ain't our problem, but he's nineteen, and I can't stop him." He stopped to pour in more coffee.

"How does that concern me?" Jim asked, genuinely puzzled.

"Well," continued the large man, "It seems I'm short a man for my farming operation this year. Francis was my hired hand, and he's gone. Fact of the matter is, he farmed that quarter-section of your mother's last year, and I was counting on him to do it again this year. Now that he's gone, I need someone to replace him. As I see it, the best man for the job has already farmed it and would most likely live right on the premises. I'd be willing to split the profits with you right down the middle, if that's alright with you. Do you need some time to think it over?"

"Not at all!" answered Jim. "Yes, that's fine with me." He offered a handshake to Parry. It was eagerly accepted.

All the way home, Jim considered and reconsidered the economics of his arrangement with Oscar Parry. Money would be tight for the coming year, he calculated. What little he and Mary had saved in Minot would help them get by. If they could just survive the coming year, he thought, they could then take back control of half of the original farm, a chunk which could provide them a decent living.

As Jim expected, Mary and Rose shared his enthusiasm about the year ahead. Finally, Jim concluded, he was on the way to doing what he was meant to do.

1929

After two days of rain and dark skies, the second Sunday of July offered sunshine and just enough breeze to keep the flies from landing on the food assembled for the Spencer Christian Church annual Sunday school picnic on the John Schoepf farm three-and-a-half miles northwest of town. Cars, trucks, buggies and the wagon used to haul tables and chairs from the church to the outdoor gathering lined the driveway. Children scurried about the yard in every direction. Several men worked to arrange the outdoor furnishings while women were quick to put coverings on the tables. One person was obviously in charge of all the activity. A tall, thin woman with red hair moved easily between the outdoor arrangements to the food preparations inside and back out again. It was her first time as a hostess, but she displayed the demeanor of a veteran. John Schoepf took a break from helping to place a table, spotted her and realized he had never been more proud of his wife. He found a glass of water, sat in his favorite rocker on the porch and reflected on how he got to this point in his life.

Gay Violet Schoepf's personality could not have been more of a contrast to that of her husband. He was a hard-core introvert while she was the ultimate extrovert. He was a thinker, and she was a doer. As the oldest of three children of a nearby farmer, Gay had a strong work ethic and was accustomed to being in charge. John grew up on a farm where a strong-minded single mother raised six children without the aid of a husband who died young. He learned to work hard but to let someone else do most of the planning and instruction. As a result, he often thought he and Gay were the perfect complementary couple. Even John's mother grudgingly came to realize that they were meant for each other.

One of the many things Bertha Schoepf had been inflexible about was diligent attendance at all services of the St. Matthew's Lutheran Church in Spencer. Each Sunday and Wednesday, she and her daughter and five sons would hitch up two buggies, dress in their very best clothes and drive the four miles south to town for services. All six of the children were easy to identify, for each had the dark piercing eyes of their mother. The boys were all considered attractive catches for any girl who could somehow get past the mother's rigid defenses. Consequently, few tried.

After most church services, Bertha would stay around to help serve coffee, cookies, cake and other treats. The church was as much of a social setting as a religious one for most attendees, so the after-service events consumed over an hour, what with clean-up to be done after the visiting had concluded. The Schoepf boys used that time to wander about the town and do some socializing of their own. Usually, they gravitated toward Main Street where Pepmueller's Pool Hall was open. Otto and Reinhold became eight-ball legends there. Each possessed a steady and accurate hand when holding a cue stick and consistently came home with more than they had wagered. The boys agreed that was a secret best kept from their mother.

One Wednesday evening in the summer of 1922, the Schoepf brothers were on their way downtown for some fun when, as they passed the Spencer Christian Church, just two blocks from their destination, twenty-one-year-old John saw a young girl seated alone in a buggy in front of the church. Feeling unusually full of himself at the moment, he urged his brothers to go on, promising to meet them shortly. Something about the girl intrigued him, and he felt the need to stop and talk to her. Sporting what he hoped was a welcoming smile, he sauntered over to the buggy.

"You look lonesome sitting there all yourself," he started.

"I'm not," the girl said without returning his smile. John looked right, then left, and saw no one else in the vicinity.

"I don't see anyone else around," he countered. Then he paused for a reaction.

"You're here, aren't you?" was her prompt reply. "Besides, my parents and brothers are inside, and they'll be along any minute."

"I don't believe I've seen you before," John continued. "Are you new in town?"

"We just moved here from LeMars, Iowa, in March," the girl offered. "We live about five miles north of town." John instantly placed the location. It was the old Bartholow farm. Jacob Bartholow had sold out and moved to town the past spring. Suddenly John realized his own shortcoming.

"Oh, I'm sorry," he said. I should probably introduce myself. My name is..."

"I know who you are," the girl interrupted. "You're one of those Schoepf boys. You live in that beautiful house we go by every time we come to town or go home." She was right, John knew. The house was one of the most immaculate in the area, thanks to his mother's drive to have the very best of everything. The Simmons brothers, a family of local carpenters, had spent much time over the years making it one of the most ornate ones around.

"Yes, I am. I'm John."

"And I'm Gay," she said. "Gay Coatsworth. "And these people you are about to meet are my parents, Will and Maude, and my little brothers, John and Milo." John turned to see a man, woman and two small boys coming down the walk in front of the church toward the wagon. Gay then introduced them all to one another, and John noticed how easily she took charge of the situation.

Over the next few weeks, John Schoepf spent less time at Pepmueller's and more time near the Spencer Christian Church. After two more not-so-random encounters with Gay Coatsworth, he worked up the nerve to ask her father for permission to call on her. The sight of him doing so amused her, she would tell him in later years. John was a man of average height, while her father was a stern-looking man of diminutive stature, yet the larger of the two was stuttering and stammering his request.

"Have you asked her?" was the terse response. John turned to Gay only to see her beaming.

Bertha Schoepf had little complaint about her sons casually dating girls who were not Lutheran. She simply didn't want any of her boys to marry outside their faith. For that reason, John knew that she would, for the present, not object to his seeing Gay Coatsworth on a regular basis. Only if matters between Gay and him went beyond regular socializing would she likely object. In the summer of 1923, that's exactly what happened.

"Do we have a future together?" Gay asked him as he drove her from Voight's Cafe back to her home on a Saturday night in August. Ironically, that topic had consumed most of his thoughts for the previous month. He knew that by all standards of the time, she was a true beauty, and he wondered what she saw in him. He was also afraid that without making a further commitment, he might well lose her to any of several other eligible men about town, maybe even to one of his brothers. He determined that he simply would not allow that to happen. Her query caused him to stop the buggy and look directly into her hazel eyes. He took both of her hands in his.

"Gay Violet Coatsworth," he said, "if your father gives his permission, will you marry me?" Her immediate response was laughter that puzzled him momentarily.

"Remember what happened the last time you asked him something like that?" she replied, still laughing. Her laughter started his. "Yes, John Schoepf, I will marry you," she finally said.

"It's her decision," was Will Coatsworth's only response. John and Gay decided that February or March of 1924 would be a good time for a wedding. That meant that there was precious little time to do oh, so many things, but one of those things loomed much larger than any other. Somehow, Bertha must be informed.

Bertha Schoepf had no difficulty with her daughter Anna marrying Wilbur Matkins, a fellow Lutheran, in 1913. Nor did she object when her oldest son , Otto, married Dora Brunken, another Lutheran, in 1914. Bill, her next son, married Ruby Simmons of the renowned local homebuilding family, in January of 1917, with the bride being seven months pregnant. That caused genuine disapproval from Bertha. The 1920 marriage of John's brother George to Emily Richards, a Methodist girl from Iowa, elicited such wrath from his mother that George and his bride immediately left Spencer for Sioux Falls on terms which remained bad for years. For the moment, John could not see how the prospect of informing his mother that he intended to marry a non-Lutheran girl just recently removed from Iowa could have a positive outcome. This, he knew, would take some thought.

After almost two weeks of agonizing pondering, John formed a plan, which was the easy part. Enacting it would take resolve he wasn't sure he possessed. Finally, one evening, he and Reinhold, his only remaining sibling still living at home, were helping their mother clear the supper table. With his brother for moral support, John addressed Bertha, whose back was toward him as she was scraping plates.

"Mother, I'm going to marry Gay Coatsworth," he said as steadily as he could. Then he braced himself for the worst.

"Is she Lutheran?" Bertha asked without pausing in her duties.

"No."

"Then I don't approve. And I won't be there." As far as John was concerned, that settled the matter. He had done his duty by informing her of his intentions. Though he had hoped for a positive response, he knew he had fulfilled his familial responsibility. He had no control over the reaction to his announcement.

The following day John informed Gay of his mother's response to his declaration. She wasn't surprised. She said she had expected it and that perhaps they should be practical about planning a wedding. Why spend much-needed money on a pageant when only the ceremony was vital, she asked. All she wanted, she said, was for them to be married and begin a life together, she said. Announcements, invitations, flowers, bridesmaid dresses—they were all a needless frivolity. What was really important were the vows they made to each other. She suggested they plan a trip to Mitchell or Sioux Falls for an afternoon wedding, then a return to Spencer to begin the next chapter of their lives.

"Will your parents go along with that?" John queried.

"When they realize how much money we will save them, they're sure to agree," she answered. An additional benefit of Gay's plan, John realized, was that Gay's parents would not be present, so Bertha should not feel unduly slighted.

On February 28, 1924, John Schoepf drove a buggy two miles north of his home and picked up his fiancée. He and Gay Coatsworth travelled five miles south on muddy roads caused by an early thaw to Spencer where they boarded a train bound for Sioux Falls. At the train station there, they were met by John's brother George and his wife Emily. George and Emily then escorted them to a nearby church and stood as best man and bridesmaid while an Episcopal minister performed a wedding ceremony. The newlyweds then returned to Spencer, retrieved their buggy and drove to Bertha's house to deliver the news.

As expected, Bertha did not accept with joy the news of her son's marriage. For that reason, John was glad that Gay had chosen to remain in the buggy while he delivered the message. Even the cold night air was preferable to what was likely to happen inside the Schoepf house.

John knew that he was dealing with a proud and stubborn woman. His mother had survived the premature death of her husband, willfully raised six children of good character, all the while managing a farm that prospered as she did so. She was an unusual force in a man's world, and she knew it.

"Gay and I went to Sioux Falls today and got married," was John's simple statement to his mother. He studied her for a reaction.

"Well, I guess that settles it then," was her unemotional response. With that, she removed her apron, turned and walked upstairs to her bedroom. Somewhat puzzled, John then returned to Gay, and they drove back to Spencer to spend their wedding night at the local hotel.

Lacking money and knowing only farming as a trade, John knew he could not, for the moment, buy farmland. Instead, he and Gay rented a farm about ten miles northwest of Spencer for the first three years of their marriage. At the end of that lease, they were still cash-strapped, so they rented their current farm. In the meantime, their household grew by two. Delma Eileen Schoepf was born in March of 1925, and Byrle Norrell joined the family in October of 1926. Gay adapted easily to motherhood, John noted. She was also not afraid to herd hogs or cattle, in addition to her household chores. She had even helped with grain threshing when needed. She was the ideal companion, John knew.

Some four months after their elopement, John and Gay were surprised to see Bertha's wagon, with Reinhold driving, rolling up their driveway. They recognized Bertha seated beside John's brother in the wagon. The back of the wagon seemed to contain furniture of some sort. John and Gay hurried out to greet the visitors. To their surprise, Bertha addressed and hugged her son and her daughter-in-law as if there had been no strain, much less break, in their relationship.

"Thought you might be in need of some furniture," Bertha stated calmly. John looked into the rear of the wagon and recognized his mother's prized dining room table with accompanying chairs, a dresser that John had used throughout most of his life and some boxes of clothing and personal items that he had neglected to take when he moved out. After the wagon was unloaded, Gay invited Bertha and Reinhold inside and offered to serve them lunch. For most of the afternoon, the four of them conversed as though nothing unpleasant had ever occurred among them. By the time Bertha and Reinhold left in mid-afternoon, all seemed well. When Bertha rose to leave, she stared first at Gay, then looked John directly into his eyes.

"You did well, son, "she said sternly. "Keep her. You need her more than you'll ever know." With that, she left. As she and Reinhold drove down the driveway, John and Gay looked at each other and breathed a huge sigh of relief.

John Schoepf watched the final arrangements for the Sunday school picnic fall into place. He reached into his pocket for a handkerchief to wipe the sweat from his forehead. After replacing the handkerchief in its designated pocket, he felt the pocket on the opposite side of his overalls to make sure he had his harmonica. It was such a joyous day, he thought, that he might entertain the crowd with his musical talents. His harmonica skills were renowned throughout the community. He began to rock slowly and rhythmically, savoring the moment, sure that life couldn't get much better. Then they came back.

They were what his mother had described as his demons. Most people had them, she said. His brother William was haunted by wanderlust, unable to stay with one job or in one place for more than a year or two. Even now, Bill and his wife Ruby, along with five small children, were in the Upper Peninsula of Michigan with Ruby's father. Bill and his father-in-law Elzie Simmons were supposedly working in a Ford factory in Kingsford that produced wooden-sided automobiles. No matter, John thought. Bill would most likely be moving on shortly. That was his way.

John's brother George seemed to be locked in never-ending combat with alcohol. He seldom seemed to win. That duel started before the falling-out with their mother. Poor Emily, his wife, did everything she could to save him from self-destruction, but most of his family believed it to be only a matter of time his demons destroyed their marriage and his body.

John's demons were not as apparent as those of his brothers, perhaps because he was somewhat naturally skilled at hiding them. They would cause him to withdraw from the world around him, expect the worst outcome from any ongoing situation and prepare himself to face that result. Because he was an introvert, few people could see when those demons haunted him. The demons, in turn, only fueled his natural personality.

John's demons, according to his mother, most likely originated with the death of his father in the late summer of 1906. As a boy, John had been more attached to his father than had any of his brothers. The two of them spent much time together and shared a love of horses still present in the younger one. John took his father's death hard. He remembered having to be carried kicking and screaming from the grave long after the funeral service ended. He also remembered wondering for a long time where his Papa was and when he would see him again.

According to Bertha, the only possible cure for that which bedeviled him lay in the Lutheran faith. Church attendance, along with earnest prayer, would rid him of his curse. For years, he believed that, and heeded his mother's advice faithfully. Lately, though, doubts had arisen. He had started to think that Gay, not God, might be the key to his salvation.

The winter of 1925 was the first time John had subjected his wife to the invisible haunting. Instead of looking forward to getting outside and moving in the warm spring weather, John seemed stuck in winter hibernation mode. He had no interest in preparing for the upcoming growing season and awoke nearly every day with a new physical malady of unknown origin. By late March, Gay had convinced him to visit Doc Tilley, son of the man who had presided over John, Sr.'s demise. Afraid of the results but wanting to please his wife, John went. Doc Tilley could find nothing wrong with him. The doctor recommended getting outside to work in the fresh air was probably the best remedy. The patient followed the advice and seemed to feel better. He also took to playing a harmonica in order to relax. He found he had a gift for playing it and often entertained small groups with his musical skill.

After the planting finished, some demons still existed. What if no rain fell? Suppose windstorms decimated his fields? What will we do if a plague of locusts is visited upon us? What if I can't provide for my wife and newborn daughter? All of these possibilities weighed heavily upon John Schoepf's mind throughout 1925, but he did the best he could to hide them from his wife. Not only did he not want to worry or disappoint her, but he really did not want to face those concerns any more. By the time the harvest was completed in November, he realized that it had been a good year. His internal fretting had been groundless after all. Then there was next year to think about.

In 1926, the thought process was repeated. By the end of the year, John once again had obvious reason to rejoice in life, but he didn't. Once more, crops and livestock thrived, and his son had been born. Rather than celebrate a successful life, though, he worried instead about 1927. He reasoned that he was about due to get a dose of humility. Prosperity comes at a price, he reckoned. After all, he had concluded, his early happiness had cost him the company of his father, who would have been 64, still relatively young, had he been alive then. His wife brought him as much joy as he had ever experienced, and his children were an absolute delight to him. Yes, John was sure that the bill for such blessings would come due any minute, and he was not sure he wanted to pay it.

John Schoepf never did play his harmonica at the Christian Church Sunday school picnic as he had planned. Instead, he rocked on the porch and watched the festivities without seeing them. By late afternoon, when people were starting to leave, he couldn't remember any of the event. He couldn't even remember eating. Even after all had departed, he still had visitors.

1934

The Stock Market crash in October of 1929 triggered the Great Depression of the 1930's a time when a fourth of the U.S. labor force was unemployed. Little, if any of those events immediately affected the people of South Dakota, though. Being mostly farmers or working in farm-related businesses, those folks had already spent most of the 1920's at the bottom of the economic totem pole. They lived in a constant economic depression. The prices farmers received for the crops and livestock they produced dropped steadily, spurring many farmers to increase production in hopes of increasing revenues and profits. That strategy not only didn't work, bur helped to create an even bigger problem.

Without thought to long term future effects, many caretakers of the soil threw caution to the wind and began to farm more and more land. More production means more income, they reasoned. They soon found themselves wrong. Their efforts resulted in more supply of the goods they produced, which, in turn, caused the prices offered farmers to plummet. Worse yet, the direct result of working all acreage and leaving no idle acres came at a time when climate conditions in the Midwestern U.S. brought about constant west and southwest winds strong enough to lift and move topsoil and prevent seed from taking root. It was commonly said that, in order to visit South Dakota, one would have to drive east to Minnesota or Iowa. What little crop remained was subjected to extreme drought. For many farmers, those conditions meant one or more years with no commodities to sell.

It was the Dust Bowl more than the Depression that caused the failure of so many South Dakota farms in the state. An estimated 50,000 residents of the state left to seek their livelihood elsewhere. The Healy family wasn't among them, but their farm was affected nonetheless. Including the parents, there were now eight mouths to feed and bodies to clothe.

While Jim and Mary Healy worked together on their 160-acre farm for some sixteen years, they also found time to expand their family. Having returned from a short time in North Dakota with one son, Joseph, they managed to add Richard, nicknamed Bud, in 1919, Eugene in 1921, Vincent in 1925, Robert in 1927 and Urban (Bus) in 1930. Even at young ages, most of the boys were recognizable by being short of stature, thick in the chest and having slightly red complexions, like their paternal grandfather, Will Healy. Bud was the only exception, being thin and lanky like the Duncan side of the family. Over time, they all displayed a very strong set of morals and an unending work ethic. Those traits, too, were inherited.

One morning in mid-June of 1934, Jim Healy finished his breakfast and decided to walk the fields he had plowed for the year. Nine-year-old Vinnie walked beside him and imitated his father whenever the elder one would stop, stoop and scoop a handful of dry soil. They would then sift through it, looking for corn seed, only occasionally finding some. That which they did find was dry and rootless. For the second straight year, the crop had failed, leaving Jim with a decision to make, and little time to do it. When he and Vinnie returned to the house, Jim told Mary that they needed to talk. She stopped the lunch preparations she was making, wiped her hands on a towel, removed her apron and accompanied her husband to the farmhouse living room. Jim looked into her eyes.

"We're not going to have a crop again this year," he said as directly as possible.

"I've been expecting to hear that," Mary replied. After a long moment of silence, she asked, "What will we do?"

"We're not going to do what we did last year," Jim answered. "We wasted time, effort and tractor fuel trying to save what amounted to nothing. This year we're going to just let it go and hope for a better next year."

"How will we get by in the meantime?" Mary wondered.

"Well, we still have the two milk cows, a few chickens and a small bunch of hogs. That, along with the garden, should get us by. Meanwhile, I thought I'd take a drive up to Salem this afternoon. There's a big crew of men building the new courthouse, and maybe I can find work there." Long moments of silence passed between the two. Eventually, Mary broke the quiet.

"I'll go along with whatever you think is best, dear. I trust you." Trusting her husband to protect the welfare of her and their family was something she learned when she begged him to leave Minot in 1918. As soon as she told him she felt unsafe there, he acted swiftly and without question in bringing her and their infant son Joseph back to South Dakota. That settled the matter as far as Jim was concerned. That afternoon, he drove the eleven miles to Salem

As Jim Healy approached the northwest corner of the county seat, he could easily see the unmistakable buzz of construction activity. Trucks were moving about in every direction with countless men and an occasional horse-drawn wagon mixed in. Jim wasn't surprised at the moving throng. He had heard that the plan called for the new three-story courthouse to be built on a tight eight-month schedule. Work had begun in April with the razing of the previous wooden structure on the same site. That allowed very little time for any kind of work stoppages due to weather or logistical problems. After parking his car two blocks away, Jim found his way to the temporary wooden shack which served as the site headquarters of the Huron Construction Company which oversaw the project under the direction of the federally-funded Works Progress Administration. The W.P.A. was created to provide work for some of the country's unemployed by putting them to work on projects that would benefit the general public. That included the erection of courthouses, bridges and the conversion of dirt roads to gravel in rural areas.

"Farmer, huh?" asked the man across the desk, staring at James over the top of a pair of reading glasses. "Is that all you've ever done?"

"No, sir. Years ago I worked on the railroad in North Dakota."

"Doing what?"

"I bossed a crew of eight that kept a stretch of tracks clear and in working order."

"Have any problems with that?"

"Other than an occasional tardy one, not really." Again, Jim watched Mr. Reading Glasses pause to think.

"Married?" the supervisor finally asked.

"Yes."

"Any children?"

"Six. All boys,"

"Still tryin' to farm?"

"Not this year," Jim said. My crop's pretty well ruined, and I'm not about to throw money I don't have after money I won't get. I do have a few chickens and hogs, though. And two milk cows. Along with a garden we water every day, we can probably get by until next year."

"What then?"

"I don't know. Hope for better times, I guess."

"In the meantime, I'd like to give you an opportunity to keep those hungry mouths fed. You've told me enough to show me you're motivated to work, and I have a need for someone to keep our supply chain moving. If we're going to finish this building on schedule, I need to know that whatever concrete, bricks, other materials and tools will be here when we need them. Based on your railroad experience and the fact that you have milk cows to tend, and they don't give you any days off, I think you may just be the man for that. What do you think?"

"What would I be doing?"

"Lots," said the supervisor. "Every day, you'll have to talk to our crew foremen to find out what they're going to need for the immediate future. Then it will be your job to get those materials ordered and see that they arrive on time. You'll be dealing with a lot of different personalities, but I'm sure you did that on the railroad."

"Yes, I did, but that was years ago."

"You're years smarter now. I'm sure it will all come back to you in short order. Besides, for $35 a week, I'm sure you can learn on the fly."

"Yes, sir," an ecstatic Jim Healy answered. The supervisor rose from his chair and extended a hand to seal the deal. Jim wasted no time in responding. The trip home seemed remarkably short.

The first thing Jim Healy learned on his new courthouse building job was that he was the sixth man in the job since work began in early April. By mid-day on his first day on the premises, he knew why. No one had applied any organization to the process. Crew leaders sometimes brushed off his efforts, saying they were too busy working in the moment to worry about tomorrow. Two of them came to him at the end of the day with requests for supplies they needed the next day, leaving Jim little if any time to contact suppliers and make last-minute delivery arrangements. He needed a system, Jim knew, so all that evening, he spent his thoughts on forming one.

On Tuesday morning, Jim located the site superintendent who hired him and informed him of what he intended to implement as soon as possible. The plan met with instant approval. Throughout the remainder of the morning, Jim informed each foreman that, henceforth, he would need to have their requests by noon of each day so he could guarantee that the materials would be available when needed. He considered implementing a 48-hour lead time policy but decided to wait until later to do that. One small step at a time, he reminded himself. After enduring some initial resistance and a healthy dose of profanity from a couple of them, he received agreement from all. By the end of his first week on the job, he could see that his system worked. Tensions between him and the crew leaders had all but vanished. Jim was happy. He was providing income for his family, and he was having fun doing it. His relief was immeasurable.

Week by week, the new McCook County courthouse took shape. The concrete walls were almost entirely hidden by the tan brick façade and decorative stones on each side. By late September, nearly all the exterior was finished and work began on the inside. Shortly, Jim saw that the high ceilings, oak finish and marble floors inside were of the highest quality. He couldn't help but think that his establishment of an orderly building supply flow had something to do with it. Any doubt about that was vanished in early December.

"I have a confession to make," the project superintendent who had hired Jim said as they once again sat across the desk from each other.

"What's that?"

"I didn't think you'd make it." He then lit a cigar, leaned back in his chair and assumed the posture of a man feeling good about success.

"What do you mean?"

"Well, you weren't the first one in the job, as I'm sure you know. There was a handful of others before you, and they all quit."

"Why was that?"

"Well, my guess is that we're mixing two totally different groups of people together here. Some of them, like me and most of the crew foremen, are construction lifers. We probably would have found work somewhere with or without a Depression. The rest, like you, are people who have probably not built anything more than an outhouse. They don't know squat about building and likely don't care. All they're interested in is the next payday. You, on the other hand, are different."

"How so?" Jim asked. The superintendent took a long drag on his cigar before responding.

"I don't really know if you give two hoots about building something.   I do know, though, that have at least a couple of qualities that I like." Another long cigar puff ensued.

"And what are those?"

"Well, for starters, you're damn good with people, and that's not easy when you're dealing with folks who all think they know more than you do. Fact is, when it comes to putting up a building, they do. That didn't stop them from working with you, though, and that's to your credit. You earned their respect by showing that you shared common goals with them and that even a beginner can have some good new ideas. You also seem to like what you're doing. Maybe that's why you're so good at it. Maybe that's why I'd like you to think about coming back to work for us next year."

"Where would that job be?" Jim asked out of genuine interest. After all, the superintendent was right on both counts. Jim had indeed earned respect and proved his skills.

"Madison," was the reply. Jim knew that the county seat of Lake County and lay about forty miles northeast of Salem, about a fifty-mile drive from the Healy farm. "We have another courthouse to build. Same type of deal, tear down an old wooden building and put up a huge one, just like here. Same schedule, too, and likely the same gang of foremen. All I'm asking you to do now is think about it."

"I certainly will!" a flattered Jim answered. For the second time in six months, he raced home. That evening, Jim, Mary and six boys drove to Montrose to pick up Jim's mother for dinner in the Rosemont Hotel dining room. The choice of what to do next year would wait. Jim Healy was just supremely happy to have one to make.

The tall red haired woman standing over John Schoepf at the kitchen table in their rented farmhouse on an early January morning was someone he had never met in almost eleven years of marriage. With both hands on the back of a chair next to his, she leaned over to give him a close look at the resolve in her face.

"You need to stop putting yourself through these spells," she commanded. "It's not fair to me. It's not fair to you, and it's certainly not fair to our children. They need more than a mother. They need a full-time father, too, not one who drifts off in silence for days or weeks at a time." John simply sat silently, not knowing what to say in response, knowing she was right. This was not the first time they had had this conversation. Each time, John wished it would be the last. He was sure Gay felt the same way. The tired firm tone in her voice hinted that this might be the final time, and John might not like the outcome.

Over a period of nearly thirty years, John had come to recognize each of the fears that plagued him. Lack of land ownership translated into lack of success. Lack of success, in turn, cast doubt in his mind about his ability to support his family, and a growing one it was. Delma and Byrle were joined in 1930 by Wilferd, who was almost immediately nicknamed Wit, dark-eyed Eleanor in 1932 and Donald in 1933. John prayed he was a good enough father to provide for them, but he was never sure.

"Count your blessings," Gay had often told her husband. "You have a loving family who has faith in you. Obviously God is watching over all of us. Trust in Him, my dear." That strategy usually worked, at least for awhile. Weeks, or maybe months later, John would relapse into a thought process of believing tragedy would soon occur. Then he would recall that his father had died surprisingly young at age 43. In less than ten years, he himself would reach that milestone. What would his family do if the same thing happened to him?

At their worst, John Schoepf's demons would leave him withdrawn from others and often incapable of making any decisions or taking any action. On those occasions, he would sometimes be unable to acknowledge the existence of his children or his wife. Gay made numerous attempts to relieve her husband of his burden, but none had succeeded. First, she had pushed him toward a complete physical examination, which resulted in Doc Tillley saying he had nothing more than a case of the nerves. He recommended that the patient undertake a short-term project with a definable near-future completion. John then went home and built a new fenced-in area for the family chickens. For a time, he seemed to be at ease and content. A few weeks later, though, he retreated into a typical state of fretting. Two weeks into that spell, he found his job with the W.P.A., and all seemed well again.

"I'm trying," John finally said to Gay. "I just don't know what to do."

"I've offered all the ideas I have," she replied. With that, she untied her apron, draped it over a chair and left the room, leaving her stunned husband alone with his thoughts.

For a long time, John sat at the kitchen table watching large and heavy snowflakes drift in abundance toward the ground. He re-filled his coffee cup reasoned that this year might indeed be a good one for farming. The more snow that fell, the more moisture that might be retained by the soil, making the soil more resistant to the relentless winds that had, until recently, relocated much of it elsewhere.

John Schoepf and his family had thus far survived The Great Depression in better shape than most South Dakotans. 1932 was a low yield and low price year for crops. Dust Bowl conditions resulted in no crops whatsoever for 1933 and 1934, so the Schoepfs survived on whatever food a large, hand-irrigated garden, along with some chickens, an occasional hog and a few cows, including two Holsteins for milking, provided. In addition, John had found work with the government-funded Works Progress Administration driving a truck delivering loads of gravel to crews of workers who were resurfacing the old dirt roads in McCook County. Twenty-five dollars a week was a windfall he couldn't pass up. After doing that throughout the spring, summer and fall of the previous two years, he was ready to return to full-time farming. By the fall of 1934, the torrential Dust Bowl winds had all but ceased in eastern South Dakota. The time seemed right.

Another blessing that helped the Schoepf family endure the Depression in solvent financial condition was, ironically, the lack of land ownership. Most farmers, including John, knew that the long-term key to financial success was to own land to be sold to a family member at some point in the future. In other words, a farmer's wealth usually manifested itself at the end of his career when his assets could be liquidated to provide for retirement. Because he owned no land, he had no retirement assets, but he also had no mortgage. Nor did he owe any real estate taxes. Those types of financial obligations had caused many a farmer to lose everything and relocate. Still, he wasn't getting any younger, and he had a responsibility to look toward an uncertain future. Sure, John had heard of something called Social Security which could ultimately provide a retirement income, but that idea at present was only a plan being pushed by President Franklin D. Roosevelt. It wasn't a reality, yet, and there was no assurance it ever would be.

John had always wanted to own his own farmland, but had never been able to come up with the financial resources to do so. That failure helped paved the way for the legions of self-doubt that often invaded his thoughts, sometimes paralyzing him. "His demons" his mother had called them. He would just have to have faith, Bertha said, that he could fend them off when needed. Until they returned, he had to believe they would not conquer him.

John sipped his coffee and began to seriously work out the details of a plan he thought would result in long-term monetary success. It was risky, to be sure, but then, what financial venture wasn't, especially in the current economic times. And he needed help, he determined, the kind of help his wife or young children could not provide. That was the big obstacle.

Quite simply, John intended to increase his farming efforts for 1935. True, the idea seemed ludicrous at first. After all, countless farmers throughout the Midwest had gone bankrupt and lost their farms in recent years, but that created an opportunity. Land could be rented cheaply, he figured. Landowners, including banks, would be as likely to rent their holdings as sell them. After all, getting some money from them was a better alternative than waiting for buyers who might never materialize. Getting land to use would be the easy part, he was sure. He could probably find as many as six quarter-sections, maybe more, to rent. To farm that much land, though, meant that he would have to find some help. He simply couldn't do it alone. With so many unemployed folks about, he figured he would have no problem finding some. In fact, he felt he could afford to be particular. He could also afford to be thrifty. "Beggars can't afford to be choosy," his mother had often preached. Surely, he thought, the opportunity he had in mind would attract numerous suitors.

John Schoepf was wrong. The first prospect he approached was his older brother Bill, who along with his wife, the former Ruby Simmons, was trying to raise a family of eight children. Bill and Ruby had spent a few years farming in northern Wisconsin and working in a Ford factory in Kingsford in the Upper Peninsula of Michigan before returning to Spencer two years ago. Bill seemed unable to put down any long roots and was always looking for a better opportunity. Their mother had said that, no matter where he was or what he was doing, Bill always had one eye on the road and was forever leaning toward it. Sure that he had a special rapport with Bill, who had also driven gravel truck for the W.P.A., John drove over to see him when the snow stopped and the roads were cleared.

Bill and Ruby Schoepf rented a farmhouse a mile south of Spencer on Highway 38, just across the road from the Spencer quarry, the point of origin for the gravel the Schoepf brothers hauled. "Just a short walk to work," Bill had sometimes quipped. He was always a good-natured one, John knew. Ruby welcomed John into their home and, without asking, poured him a cup of coffee. "Go fetch Papa," Ruby ordered young Elzie, the namesake of his maternal grandfather. John watched the boy scurry off toward the living room. Momentarily, Bill appeared.

"'Mornin', brother," Bill greeted in his normally gravelly voice through his customary grin that advertised him as the one Schoepf brother who knew how to find fun in any situation. "What brings you around on a cold winter day?"

"Somethin' I want to ask you about. I have an idea I need some help with."

"Shoot," responded Bill as he poured himself a cup of coffee and joined John at the table.

"I'm thinking about renting some extra acres this year, a lot of them. But if I do that, I'm going to need some help. I can't farm much more than a half-section by myself."

"How much more?

"Maybe a couple of sections. They'd be scattered, though. I doubt I can find that much land in one piece."

"You're probably right," said Bill. "Even if you did, I don't know if two guys can handle it. And you'd need another tractor. That's a big investment."

"Yeah, you're right. It is a gamble. But I can rent the land for a portion of the crop to minimize the risk. I wouldn't have a mortgage, so the only thing I'd have to borrow money for is another tractor, and I might be able to make some sort of a trade for that."

"What would you trade?"

"Horses, maybe."

"Ah, you and your horses," Bill countered. "You're just like Papa. He was always fiddle-fartin' around with horses, buying, selling, trading, mostly just for the fun of it. And he was good at it, too. So are you. You're probably right. I'm sure you have two or three that could get you a used tractor. O.K., so what do you need from me?"

"First off, your opinion. Do you think the idea will work?"

"Could."

"Do you want in on it with me?"

"Can't help you there, brother. Ruby and I decided that I'll drive the gravel truck again this year. Might be the last chance. The money's good, and the work is easier than farming."

"What about Merle?' John was referring to Bill's oldest son, who was a few weeks from turning eighteen.

"I suppose you could ask him," Bill replied. "I doubt he'd be interested. He's never been much for doing farm chores. Or any other work, for that matter. Besides, he's been workin' at Burnham's lumber yard recently. I hope they get more out of him than I do. I swear sometimes the boy drives me crazy on purpose."

"Mama said you did the same thing to Papa," John answered.

"You're probably right. That's probably what she meant when she says that what goes around comes around. Say, what about Ott's boy Glenn?"

The idea intrigued John. He knew that Glenn was the same age as Merle and didn't think that the boy had a job. He told Bill he would go see Ott and, hopefully, Glenn. He and Bill parted company and John made his way into Spencer to find his oldest brother, the town constable and chief maintenance man. By the middle of the afternoon, John and Glenn had reached an agreement. As soon as planting season began, Glenn would work after school, where he was a senior, Monday through Friday and all day on Saturdays. Once school was out for the year, the young man would move in with his uncle's family and would earn a dollar a day, plus room and board.

The finishing touch on John Schoepf's plan to ensure farming success for 1935 involved trading a pair of cherished draft horses to Elmer Kreutzfeldt who lived four miles west of town for a four-year-old Allis-Chalmers tractor. Meanwhile he secured rental agreements for a portion of the crop proceeds rather than a flat monetary amount, to six quarter-sections of land to farm. It wasn't quite as much as he wanted, but, in addition to the two he was already farming, he had enough to test his theory.

For the first time in his life, John Schoepf had ample reason to consider himself a success. Only a few Dust Bowl winds made their way through eastern South Dakota, and those showed up mainly in April before crops were planted and September when the crops were nearing maturation. Thus, by early fall, John knew he'd done right by his family. By mid-December, he was counting just over three times his normal profit. He resolved to use the same plan for 1936 with an eye toward expanding his operation even more. Glenn had already agreed to return. The future loomed brightly.

1936 was even more profitable, largely because John added another half-section to his workload. Gay and his growing family, especially Delma and Byrle, took on more responsibility for Wit, Eleanor and Don. Wit, in particular, demanded special attention. He had an insatiable curiosity. That, coupled with no fear of the unknown, led him anywhere and everywhere. He also possessed the same disarming smile and charm as his Uncle Bill. For that reason, John and Gay were especially watchful of him. Mischievousness was one thing, he parents realized and appreciated, but they worried that his lack of an attention span might lead him to the same wanderlust lifestyle of Bill and Ruby, who had yet to settle in one locale or house for more a year or two.

By 1937, Glenn had enlisted in the army, leaving John short of help. After much consideration and discussion with Gay, they agreed that eleven-year-old Byrle was old enough to take on an adult role in the Schoepf family farming operations. Gay balked at the idea but relented when John instructed the boy in operating a tractor and had him demonstrate his skills to his mother. Byrle was mature beyond his age, attentive and cautious, the traits he needed to succeed in calming his mother. He was also an analytical thinker and problem-solver, characteristics John knew could be useful. The boy was ready, John determined.

For four more years, through 1941, John's plan worked spectacularly. Each year yielded enough profit to allow him to put money aside to realize his biggest professional dream. By December of that year, with war looming on the American horizon, he was ready to make his move. Fighting troops would need food, he knew, and American farmers would be called upon to produce that food. He intended to be one of them and to prosper from that endeavor. He bought a half-section farm with plans to farm it, along with as many rented acres as he could handle. Over time, his self-doubt demon disappeared, leaving only its "early death" companion in his psyche. John kept himself as busy as possible to keep that one at bay.

1945

In mid-April, twenty-year-old Vinnie Healy, fourth son of Jim and Mary Healy, had his world in order. His older brothers had gone on to pursue their own interests and careers. Joe and Bud had bought their own farms, and Gene had moved to Utah to realize his dreams of teaching in a high school. That left Vinnie as his father's chief assistant in operating the family farm. Younger brothers Bob and Bus did their share of the work, while eight-year-old Jerry was just growing into his.

Since graduating high school two years earlier, young Vinnie's routine was predictable. Morning milking was followed by field work and machine maintenance, then evening milking. Then, at least two nights a week were devoted to going to Canistota to see a certain young woman who had caught his fancy at a military benefit dance three years earlier.

Virginia "Toby" Bergen was short of stature with red hair and freckles that would allow her to pass for being Irish instead of the Norwegian she was. Her eyes danced as she talked, and Vinnie could not resist the urge to return again and again for more of her company. Their personalities meshed instantly, and within a year, they began to plan their future together. The only unknown in their plans was the ongoing world war. Vinnie's military draft status was uncertain, and neither of them wanted to have a life as newlyweds interrupted by military service. That belief was tragically reinforced in 1944 when Toby's brother Norman died when the bomber he was flying was shot down over Germany. Bad enough to lose a brother in war, she said, but worse to lose a husband. Vinnie agreed.

As he worked to attach a plow to a tractor in preparation for planting season, Vinnie stopped for a moment to wipe the sweat from his brow and look up at the sky. The sun was past the noon mark, he noticed, about time for lunch. He lay down his wrench and walked toward the road to see if the daily mail had arrived. It had. Glancing through it, he saw a copy of the weekly *Canistota Clipper* with a large headline reading, **War in Europe Winding Down**. That was good news, he reckoned. That left only Japan to be conquered, and that, too seemed, to be only a matter of a short time. Likely, he wouldn't be drafted, and he and Toby could proceed with their plans. Then he saw the postcard. It was addressed to him.

You are instructed to report to the Courthouse of McCook County in Salem, South Dakota, at 8:00 a.m. on Monday, May 14, in accordance with the Selective Service Act of the United States. At that time, you will be inducted into the United States Army for a period not to exceed two years in length. If you are unable to do so, you must show cause no later than that time. Failure to comply with the instructions provided in this notice may result in arrest and prosecution.

That was the entire message-short and simple. With just a post card in the mail, Vinnie Healy's world changed dramatically.

Vinnie knew he would have to make an unplanned visit to Canistota that evening. What he didn't know was how he would break the news to Toby or what effect it would have on their plans. All afternoon he searched for words that would cushion the blow for both of them. By the time he had finished supper and aimed the family Chevy toward town, he still had no idea. As he drove through town to the Bergen house, a plan occurred to him.

Canistota, like many small-but-not-tiny towns, had a movie theater that served as a welcome and thriving source of entertainment for a community that worked hard for a living. The theater showed recent release films, sometimes double features, and offered all the amenities of similar facilities in Sioux Falls and metropolitan areas. As Vinnie drove past it, he noted that the film of the evening was a Roy Rogers western titled "The Man from Oklahoma". He was thankful it wasn't a war movie. Perhaps a couple hours of a good western would relax him and Toby in preparation for the news he had to deliver. Then he realized that that wasn't his style. Straightforward and direct was his way, and he would have to trust it to work for him.

While waiting in the Bergen living room, Vinnie carried on small talk, not one of his favorite pastimes, with Toby's parents, Walter and Rose. The Bergens had recently moved into Canistota from a nearby farm and operated one of the local motels. In fact, it was one of a disproportionate number in town that prospered from the presence of the nationally renowned Ortman Chiropractic Clinic. People travelled from the far corners of the United States to be treated there, and when they arrived, they need a place to stay. A dozen local entrepreneurs were glad to oblige.

After a few minutes, Toby appeared, and she and Vinnie left. As soon as she was situated in the passenger seat, Vinnie wordlessly handed her the postcard he had just received. He sat in silence watching her study it. She read each side several times as if she were looking for some reason to dismiss it as a hoax. Finding none, she handed it back to him without saying a word. Then she stared straight ahead out the windshield. For several awkward minutes, neither said anything.

"I wish I had better news," Vinnie finally said. Toby continued to look forward. "I'm sorry."

"Why?" she responded. "It's not your fault. I guess we both knew that it could happen." Vinnie saw tears welling in her eyes and knew they would soon be overflowing. He moved toward her and slipped an arm around her shoulders.

"What does this do to our plans?" Vinnie asked hesitantly. Again, there was a long pause before she spoke.

"It means we'll just have to wait until you get home," she finally answered. She then turned to look directly into his eyes. He saw that her normal pixie-like expression was gone, replaced by a serious one that left no doubt about her intent. "And you WILL come back, Vinnie Healy." Her continued stern stare punctuated her statement.

"Yes, you bet," was his answer. He wondered if she could sense the relief that suddenly washed over him.

For the next month, Vinnie spent as much time as he could with Toby. They went to movies and for walks on nice spring evenings. Sometimes they just sat in the car and talked. During all that time, though, he was careful not to broach the subject of war, much less the possibility of him being in the middle of one. Instead, they continually reviewed the plans they had for the future. They would marry as soon as he was home for good, find a farm to rent and begin raising a family. Someday they would buy a large farm and sit in leisure watching their numerous children do most of the work. Six or seven sons should be about right, he mused aloud one evening.

"What about girls?" Toby asked, feigning indignance. "What's wrong with them?"

"Oh, nothing," Vinnie said in defense. "It's just that boys make better farmers, like my brothers and me."

"We might just have to see about that," she countered. Mutual smiles ended the conversation for the moment.

Shortly before 8 a.m. on May 14, Vinnie Healy reported to the McCook County Courthouse in Salem to enlist in the United States Army. Eighteen other young men, none of whom he knew, accompanied him when they boarded a train bound for the army enlistment center in Minneapolis, Minnesota. That was the first time Vinnie had been out of South Dakota, and he concluded that he really hadn't missed much. Most of western Minnesota had the same rolling farm fields of eastern South Dakota. Only when the train began the last eighty miles of its journey to the Twin Cities did the terrain change. From Mankato onward, the rolling hills, trees and the winding Minnesota River provided a new vista for the recruits from the prairie. By the time the train reached its destination, Vinnie realized he had seen some extremely productive farmland.

Upon arriving in Minneapolis, Vinnie and his companions were greeted by a soldier in uniform and ushered to a bus which took them to a local hotel. At the hotel they were issued room assignments, two recruits to a room, and meal tickets for the hotel's restaurant. The tickets were good for dinner and the following morning's breakfast. The fresh soldiers were also instructed to be prepared to depart the hotel, luggage in hand, at 8 o'clock the following morning, bound for the National Guard Armory.

When Vinnie arrived at the enlistment center the next day, he saw nearly a hundred young men like him. Most had a look of apprehension on their faces, and Vinnie was sure he looked the same to them. A short time later, all of them were sent to a large auditorium where, in unison, they took the oath of office to join the United States Army. Then they were sorted into groups where they were given physical examinations. A handful, he noticed, were dismissed due to one or more disqualifying physical characteristics. Most, however, were finally cleared for duty and herded on a train destined for Wichita Falls, Texas, for nine weeks of basic training.

After the train passed through Minnesota and Iowa farmland that looked much the same as South Dakota, Vinnie found himself staring out the window at the forested hillsides of southern Missouri. He guessed that that was what the Black Hills must look like. Odd, he thought, that as a lifelong resident of South Dakota, he had not ever been to the Black Hills.

"Ain't much like MCook County, is it?" Vinnie heard. He turned to see a smiling speaker he recognized as one who had boarded the train in Salem two days earlier.

"No, no it isn't," Vinnie answered. "Got a few more trees."

"Even without 'em, I bet it'd be tough to farm, wouldn't it?"

"With all those hills, I'd say so." The man then extended his right hand toward Vinnie. "Stuby," he said. "Richard James. Or, just plain ol' R.J. From Spencer".

"Vinnie Healy from Montrose," Vinnie replied, returning the handshake and feeling relieved to have someone with something in common to talk with on the last day of the voyage.

As the train snaked through Missouri, then angled southwest into Oklahoma, Vinnie and R.J. saw the land look more and more like the northern plains farmland they were accustomed to. The only difference was the occasional machine that reminded them of the grasshoppers farmers loathed. Those metal beasts were oil rigs, they were told, and the fact that the rigs were in vertical motion meant that they were pumping out oil and had been throughout the war.

By late afternoon on the second day, the rookie soldiers had crossed the Red River into Texas and, finally, the Wichita, and found themselves in Wichita Falls. They were then assigned quarters and sent to the mess hall for supper. The rest of the evening was free, so Vinnie began a letter to his parents and another to Toby, hoping they all knew not to expect long reports from him. His available time to write would be short, he reasoned, and he knew that his interest in putting pen to paper would be likewise.

The following morning, reveille awakened Vinnie and the other beginners at 5:30 a.m., his normal rising time. Instead of cows to milk, though, he had to report to the mess hall again for breakfast, then to an armory for another round of physical examinations from doctors who prodded, poked and questioned endlessly. He wondered if the war could be won simply by subjecting the enemy to the same treatment. Perhaps then immediate surrender would be inevitable. One blessing did result from the ordeal. Vinnie was informed that he had flat feet, enough that he was unfit for combat duty. He would hence be assigned to a division of combat engineers and likely be working with machinery, a passion of his and one he would, for the moment, be silent about for fear of ruining a good thing. R.J. Stuby was destined for infantry training and, following nine weeks of basic training, would be sent to Fort Benning, Georgia, for what the army called AIT—Advanced Individual Training. R.J. said he **actually** looked forward to it.

Every day for nine weeks, regardless of weather, drill sergeants pushed, pushed and pushed some more to turn farm boys and city boys alike into soldiers. The demanding physical conditioning was relentless and monotonous, but Vinnie found himself in better shape than he could have imagined. The unforgiving summer sun of north Texas made him more muscular and durable than he had ever been. Still, he was glad to be finished with it. He was anxious to find out where he would be posted next.

Geiger Field, Spokane, Washington was what the destination line next Vinnie's name on the list posted on the message board outside his barracks. He was to report for duty there on August 13, giving him a month's furlough with absolutely no doubt about where he would spend it. Within two hours, he was on a train to South Dakota. No minute of furlough time would be wasted if he could help it.

Knowing where their son's thoughts and heart were, Jim and Mary Healy had arranged for the Bergen family to pick up Vinnie at the train depot in Bridgewater, the closest one to home. The Healys would then come to Canistota an hour or so later to greet their son and enjoy a picnic supper. Vinnie was surprised and elated to see his welcoming party and appreciative of his parents for arranging it.

On his first full day home, Vinnie arose at his normal 5:30 a.m. and helped his father with the milking chores. Then, after breakfast, instead of offering to help with the haying in progress, he asked his father if he could borrow the family Chevy. Jim was quick to agree.

"Little early to go to town, isn't it?" Jim teased. "Doesn't she have any chores to do?"

"We could sure give her some," Bob added, grinning as he did.

"I could show her how to clean out some calf pens," said Bus, through the same impish smile.

"S'pose she could fling a few bales for us?" Bob asked.

"She probably wouldn't complain as much as you guys do," Vinnie finally said. "If talkin' got the work done, you guys would have been finished last week."

Instead of driving to Canistota, Vinnie pointed the car toward Sioux Falls. His plan for the day required a store neither Montrose, Canistota nor Salem had. Once there, he found a jewelry store, looked over its selection of goods and made a purchase. Then he returned home, rehearsing a speech that he hoped would work to his advantage.

That evening, Vinnie drove to Canistota to pick up Toby to take her to the county fair in Salem. She greeted him with a smile and a kiss that nearly wiped out all memory of being away for two months. As she grabbed a sweater and started for the door, though, he stopped her and asked if her father was home.

"Yes," she said. "Why?"

"I-I'd like to talk to him for a minute."

"Why?" Her smile suggested that he was not about to surprise her.

"I'd just like to. Please?" She left the room to find Walter and soon returned with him.

"Yes, Vinnie? You wanted to see me?"

"Yes, sir, I do."

"What about?" Walter, too, was half-smiling, as if he, too, knew what was about to happen.

"If it's alright with you, sir, I'd like to marry your daughter." Vinnie then waited for Walter's response. The churning in his stomach intensified. Walter remained silent, rubbing his chin in thought.

"And what does Frances say about that?" the older man finally asked. Vinnie felt his jaw drop in fear. Did he hear what he thought he had heard? He was stunned into silence. Finally, he saw Walter grin. "After all, she is most likely going to be the maid of honor, isn't she?" After a hearty laugh, he added, "Of course, it's alright with me, but you probably better ask Virginia."

"Yes!" Toby blurted out even before Vinnie could ask the question. With that, Vinnie pulled out the ring he had bought and placed it on her left hand. Only on the way to Salem did he finally remember to propose to her, and that was just because he wanted to hear her answer again.

Relieved that the fighting in the world's second Great War, was over, Vinnie Healy reported to Geiger Field in Spokane in mid-August knowing only that he was assigned to the Air Corps Engineering School. He had no idea what he would be doing, but within a day, he was informed that he would be learning to operate a drag line, something he had heard of but knew nothing about. His mission was part of an effort to prepare the air base to handle the shipment of more supplies to troops and ships in the Asian theater. Even though Japan had surrendered and fighting had stopped, the United States still maintained a military presence there, and those folks needed supplies flown from the states. More air facilities were needed, and some of those were being constructed at Geiger.

A drag line is a large piece of machinery designed to move large quantities of earth in large parcels. The payload end is a huge scoop which is placed on one end of the substance to be moved. That bucket is attached to cables which run to an arm some twelve to twenty-five feet long. The drag line operator uses a hydraulic series of levers to lift the arm so that it extends vertically. As that happens, the scoop is drug along the ground, filling as it goes. When full, the operator lifts the bucket and uses more levers to swing the bucket to one side or the other. Finally, when the bucket is in place, the operator uses more levers to release the load. Then the process is repeated until the excavation is finished.

After a half-day of standing in the cab of the drag-line cockpit watching, Vinnie was allowed to try running it on his own. The job required steady nerves and a certain element of fearlessness, two traits which were natural to him. After all, he figured, it was just like running farm machinery, just a little bigger. As a result, he learned quickly how to run the machine and that he liked doing so. It seemed to him that this military thing might be more fun than he thought.

December of 1945 turned out to be a time of change. Shortly after Thanksgiving, Vinnie was informed that the building efforts at Geiger Field were nearing an end and that he and other construction personnel would be assigned elsewhere beginning in January of 1946. Hoping that he would not he sent overseas and that he would be allowed to work outside again, he opened the envelope containing his orders and found that he was assigned to the Rapid City Air Base in Rapid City, South Dakota, only a seven-hour train ride from home. He hoped his good fortune would allow him some weekend pass time to spend with Toby.

Rapid City Air Base turned out to be the right place at the right time and the wrong job. Instead of working outdoors, Vinnie was assigned to office duty. He discovered he would be spending his days typing up personnel reports from handwritten forms provided by officers. That duty revived unpleasant memories of sophomore year typing class at Montrose High School where he finally decided that he would risk wearing out only his forefingers on the keyboard. The others would be spared for more interesting activities like milking cows. As if that weren't tortuous enough, his desk was located right next to a window, giving him only visual access to the outdoors where he wished to be. There was one offsetting blessing.

While in Rapid City, Vinnie's work schedule called for him to work weekdays and have weekends to himself. He soon found out that "weekend" furlough passes didn't necessarily mean they were exclusively for weekends. Within just a few weeks of arriving in Rapid City, Vinnie mastered the art of getting a 3-day "weekend " pass which allowed him the luxury of one five-day home visit each month. By September, though, the base commander decided to halt that practice. That was about the time that Vinnie found out he would be discharged at the end of November.

Fighting a war on two fronts separated by half the globe created a tremendous financial strain upon the United States. The national debt hadn't existed before the Depression. That's when the federal government began to borrow huge quantities of money to create jobs and pull the country up by its economic bootstraps. The onset of war in 1941 increased the amount of money that had to be borrowed. When the war ended, several debt-reducing measures, including early discharge from military service, were implemented. Vinnie Healy was a beneficiary of that idea.

Upon reaching home in early December, Vinnie found Toby and her family in frenzied preparation for a December 30 wedding. He immediately sized up the situation as organized chaos and elected to stay out of the way, while making his willingness to help known. When a high-speed train is rolling through the area, he thought, it's best to stand aside. If the train wants you aboard, it will stop for you.

To occupy his time while the wedding arrangements were being made, Vinnie jumped back into helping run the Healy farm. Every morning, he would arise at 5:30 and help his father with the milking. Jim was grateful for the assistance. Bob, who had formerly handled that responsibility, had recently moved to town to work in the shop at Montrose Implement. One morning, after the cows had been placed in their stanchions, Jim Healy posed a question of his son.

"What do you plan to do to support yourself and Toby after you're married?"

"I haven't decided yet. I have some army money saved up, so we have some time to figure that out. Maybe find some kind of job in town, just so long as it's not always inside."

"Ever think about full-time farming?" Jim asked.

"Lots," Vinnie answered. "But I don't have the money to get started."

"What if you didn't need it?"

"What do you mean?"

"I'm not gettin' any younger, you know, and the older I get, the harder it is for me to keep up with all the work around here.

With Bob gone, Bus helps out more, and Jerry does as much as he can, but next year there's going to be more to do." The older Healy paused and looked directly at Vinnie.

"How so?" A confused Vinnie asked. "You're not retiring, are you?"

"Not totally. But Clifton Jacobs did."

"So?"

"You know, son, I've kind of made it a mission to buy back that quarter section just east of the house. It was a part of the original Healy farm, and your grandmother sold it in 1918 because she had no one to help her work it. Your mother and I were in North Dakota and my brothers and sisters had either moved away or didn't want the life of a farmer. When we moved back from Minot, I made it a mission to put the farm back together. Every winter for almost thirty years, I'd go see that ornery old cuss and ask him to sell it to me. Every year he said "no" until I almost gave up. Last week I decided to give it another try, and he surprised me by saying "yes". There's nothing your mother and I would like more than for you and Toby to rent the farm from us. Bus and Jerry and I would help you work it. What do think?" Vinnie took several moments to digest what he had just heard.

"Where would we live?" Vinnie asked his father.

"Right here," Jim replied. "Your brothers and I are going to move to town into your grandmother's house. You and Toby can live here as our wedding gift to you." Vinnie remembered his grandmother Rose, who had died almost ten years earlier, and her house in Montrose. It was certainly large enough and adequately comfortable for four people. "So, what do you say, son? If you want to ask Toby about it before giving me an answer, I understand."

Later that morning, Vinnie raced the Chevy toward Canistota, anxious to present his fiancé with the offer his father had made.

"Yes!" she said, again.

On December 30, Vincent Healy married Virginia Bergen at St. Patrick's Catholic Church in Montrose. Bob Healy stood as his brother's best man while Frances Bergen served as her sister's maid of honor. An old journey continued as a new one began.

1948

Wilferd "Wit" Schoepf's life was as nearly perfect as he could ask for in late May. As he rode in a car with his uncle Ott and cousin Glenn from Spencer to Montrose for the season-opening game of the 1948 Corn Belt League baseball season, only his nerves bothered him. He hoped he would be up to the assignment he had been given.

Only a week earlier, at practice, he learned that he would be the starting shortstop for the Spencer Cardinals amateur baseball team, one of the better teams in the league. He would be displacing Glenn, who was moved over to third base. Normally that would be an awkward situation, but the decision was announced by Ott, the team manager. Probably because it was a family matter as well as a competitive one, Glenn seemed alright with the change and, in fact, was helpful to Wit.

During each mile of the twenty-mile trip from Spencer to Montrose, Wit prayed that he would not do something that would cost the favored Cardinals a game they should win. Ott had told him that he couldn't remember anyone that young playing in the league in the thirty years he had been involved with it.

"Wheeler's going to be pitching for Montrose tonight," Ott said as they passed the Highway 81 junction by Salem. "He has a sneaky fastball that looks better because of his curve. The curve doesn't break sharp, but it breaks down so it's hard to adjust to. If he gets ahead of you in the count, he'll toy with you by reversing his pitch selection. That's his problem, though. He sometimes has trouble throwing that first strike. Just look for your pitch and don't worry about hitting. You're in the lineup because of your glove."

The setting for Wit's Corn Belt League debut was ideal. The Montrose ballpark sat in the northeast corner of town across the Vermillion River from the city park. The well-groomed grass infield and outfield were surrounded by trees and a snow fence and numerous light poles. The grandstand behind home plate was freshly painted and half-full of spectators when they arrived shortly after six for a 7 o'clock game. Only when infield practice began did Wit began to relax some.

Ott was right about Wheeler being a good pitcher. He retired the Cardinals in order in the first two innings and made it look easy in the process. Glenn Duxbury, the Spencer pitcher, matched his results. In the top of the third, Wit came to bat with two outs. He scraped and dug his right foot into the back of the batter's box and waited for that first pitch. Probably going to be a curve, he guessed, so he leaned ever so slightly toward home plate. Wheeler released the ball and Wit saw it coming toward his mid-section. He waited patiently for it to break toward the plate. It didn't. At the last instant, he leaned backwards, stumbled and fell on his backside.

"Welcome to the Corn Belt League, kid," the unnamed Montrose catcher growled at the skinny figure sitting in the dirt outside the batter's box. Wit looked toward the Spencer dugout and saw that even his teammates were laughing. So much for initiation, he told himself and returned to the box to hit. Three late-breaking curveballs followed, and each was greeted by a lunging swing from someone whose left foot was striding toward third base with each effort to hit the ball. His next trip to home plate in the fifth inning resulted in another strikeout on three straight fastballs while he waited to see another curve.

By the top of the eighth, the Cardinals had carved out a 2-0 lead against Wheeler and the Irish. Wit came to bat with two outs and runners on second and third, a chance to drive in his first run as a Cardinal. Before he walked to the plate, Ott motioned him toward the third base coaching box and told him to just relax. "Try to just swing and not think too much," he counseled his nephew. Two curveballs and a fastball later, Wit returned to the bench to get his glove.

The tenuous lead remained in place going into the bottom of the ninth. After the leadoff hitter struck out, the next batter walked, and the following one advanced him with a double to right center field. Two runners in scoring position and two outs to get, Wit told himself as we watched Lloyd Hetland, the clean-up hitter stride to the plate. Ott had told Wit that Hetland used all fields as his hitting zone, so he would have to play him straight away without cheating to either side. When the count reached two balls and no strikes, he moved a step to his right, expecting Hetland to try to pull the pitch to left field. As Duxbury released the pitch, he knew instantly he had guessed wrong. A bullet of a line drive scorched its way toward left centerfield. Instinctively, Wit crossed his right leg over his left and dived in the direction of the ball. He felt it hit the webbing of his glove, reached for it with his left hand and closed it tightly. Without hesitation, he leaped to his feet to check the runner on third, who decided not to advance. Spitting out dirt, Wit tossed the ball to the pitcher and resumed his position. Even the partisan Montrose fans had to applaud such a play.

Obviously tired, Duxbury walked the next batter, loading the bases. Ott called timeout to talk to his pitcher. Assured by Duxbury that he had enough energy left in his arm to finish the game, Ott returned to the dugout. On a 2-2 pitch, the Cardinal pitcher threw the best curveball he could muster and watched as a sharp ground ball shot its way between shortstop and third base. Moving to his right with the pitch, Wit snared the ground ball after its second hop, tossed it Glenn at third base and watched Glenn's throw to first complete the game-ending double play. Ott was the first to rush out of the dugout to Wit as the final out call was made.

"If you can field like that every game, I don't give a damn if you never hit," he said. The ride back to Spencer was a joyous one.

Wit's success at catching a baseball surprised no one. He was one of those rare individuals who had a knack for instant success at any sport involving a ball. As an eighth-grader at school in Farmer, he was a starting guard for the varsity basketball team. Because Farmer didn't offer football or baseball, he turned to a form of softball called kitten ball. He starred in that, too.

Athletic success was not the only natural talent for John and Gay Schoepf's second son. He possessed a boundless curiosity and boyish innocence dressed in an easy smile that extricated him from many a precarious situation. One spring when his father was in one of his withdrawn moods and falling behind on the farm work that needed to be done, Wit decided to help older brother Byrle with the disking. He and friend Kenny Matkins, devised a way to connect the disc to the family car. The sight of a huge cloud of dust rising from a nearby field quickly jerked John from his emotional doldrums to put a stop to such folly. The father jogged toward the field, motioned for Wit to stop the car then walked up to the driver's window, which was already rolled down. Wit could see the veins in his father's neck standing out underneath the red in his face. He greeted that sight with a disarming smile before his father could say a word.

"I know, I know," Wit said. "But look, Dad, we're almost done." He continued grinning at his father, who was suddenly without words. The elder Schoepf simply turned and walked back toward the house. As he did, Wit thought he saw a hint of a smile on his father's face.

Following the win over Montrose, the Spencer baseball team continued its schedule of practicing on Wednesday and Saturday evenings. Those were the nights that most people who lived out of town came to shop and socialize. Many of them made a habit of coming to the ballpark to watch the Cardinals prepare for their Friday and Sunday league games. One of those people in particular caught Wit's eye.

One Wednesday evening during a scrimmage, Wit was almost beheaded by a line drive because he was looking intently at a young lady with the same black hair and dark eyes as her father. Wit knew who Lucille Duly was, for the two of them shared a set of cousins, though they were not directly related. Lucille's mother, also named Lucille, was the sister of Ruby Schoepf, the wife of Wit's uncle Bill, his father's brother. Therefore, all ten children of Bill and Ruby were Wit's cousins by way of their father, and Lucille's cousins through Lucille's mother.

Wit had seen Lucille in years past whenever she and her family came from Buffalo, New York, for part of a summer to visit Ruby and Bill. Lucille's mother had spent part of her youth in Spencer and had even attended the Farmer School in a nearby community, just as Wit and his siblings did. Though they lived closer to Spencer than Farmer, the school district lines put them in the Farmer district.

Lucille's family included not only her mother, but her sister Priscilla and her brother Leslie, namesake of their father Les. Wit always dismissed Leslie as a bookworm type with little social adeptness and even less athletic skill. Les, the father, was someone always with a plan for making big money. None of them seemed to work, though. Many of the Spencer locals referred to him as "Augie", a shortened version of August Wind, the kind that is nothing but constant hot air. He and Bill got on well together probably because, as Wit's father had remarked, Bill, too, was a schemer. "Some folks are thinkers, and some are doers," John had said. "Bill and Les are the first kind, but not the second."

Wit was still distracted when while waiting in the on-deck circle for his turn at batting practice he knew he desperately needed. Something about Lucille Duly looked different this year. She no longer reminded him of the pig-tailed girl he would sit behind in the Spencer Christian Church just so he could be sneaky about pulling her hair. Before stepping up to the plate, he turned to look at her and flash her a smile of recognition. She returned one of her own.

When practice was over, Wit saw that, unlike the rest of the crowd, Lucille was in no hurry to leave. Instead, she slowly walked over to the fence behind the Cardinal dugout, watching him change from his baseball spikes to his work boots. Her close presence made lacing and tying his boots an inexplicable exercise in clumsiness.

"Not often a boy is allowed to play with men, is it, Wit Schoepf."

"Only if he's good enough."

"Are you?"

"The manager says so."

"Maybe I'll just have to come out to your next game and see for myself," she said through another smile. Then she turned and walked away.

The following Friday night's game was at home against the Salem Cubs. True to her word, Lucille and her sister were clearly visible in the grandstand throughout the entire game. They were treated to another pair of fielding gems by Wit, along with his first hit. In the fifth inning, with the count two balls and no strikes, he mustered as much force as he could when he saw what looked like a fastball over the middle of the plate. His swing resulted in a dribbler that found its way in a spot on the field where the pitcher, first baseman and second baseman could not quite get to it to make a play. As he stood at first base catching his breath and wiping sweat off his forehead, his cousin Glenn, who was coaching at first asked, "Do you know where to go from here?" Wit could only smile and point to second base.

After Spencer's 7-2 win, Wit saw the fans, except for Lucille Duly, depart. Instead of leaving, she again made her way down to the fence behind the dugout as Wit was again changing his footwear.

"Guess the manager's right," she said. "You looked pretty good out there tonight."

"Thanks," he replied. "You do, too." He followed that with a question that betrayed what had been on his mind for the past 48 hours. "Would you like to go downtown for a Coke or something?" She paused before answering.

" Sure," she finally said. One Coke followed the first. Then Wit and Lucille began to go to Mitchell for an occasional movie, to Salem for the county fair and sometimes nowhere but the Spencer

City Park with hamburgers, fries and more Cokes. Within weeks, Wit realized that the Lucille Duly he used to know as a girl was now a mature woman. He hoped she saw him as a young man and not the impish boy who used to yank on her hair in church.

By mid-August, Wit knew he didn't want Lucille to return to New York with her family. He had to convince her to stay in Spencer and that it would be difficult. She had told him that she had a job waiting for her in Clarence, just east of Buffalo, writing news stories and advertising copy for a twice-weekly newspaper. Nearly desperate, he put a hastily formed plan into action.

"Do you really have to go back to Buffalo?" Wit asked Lucille one balmy evening in the city park.

"Why not?" Wit saw a half-smile on her face.

"I mean, we don't have to b-b-stop seeing each other, do we?"

"What do you mean?" Wit took a deep breath before responding.

"I mean I want you to stay here," he blurted out.

"Don't you have to go back to school?" She was referring to his second year at Dakota Wesleyan University in Mitchell where he had recently completed his first year of undergraduate work.

"I'm not going back," he said.

"Why not?"

"School is an indoor thing, and I'm an outdoor person. I'd rather work on the farm than be inside a classroom all day. Besides,

I didn't know what I wanted to study besides basketball. That's the only reason I went there."

"Have you told your folks?"

"Yeah."

"And what did they say?"

"They surprised me by agreeing. Mom knows I can't sit still in a classroom for long, and Dad knows he could use the help."

"And what would I do while you're farming?" Lucille asked.

"I don't know, maybe find a job in town. We have a newspaper, too, you know. If you're good with numbers, you could probably find an office job somewhere."

"Then what?"

"I'm hoping we can kind of save up some money and get married."

"Why, Wit Schoepf, are you proposing to me?"

"Yes, I guess I am," Wit said. "I mean, I don't have a ring or anything like that yet, but I promise I'll get you one as soon as I can."

With a simple "I accept" from Lucille, a bond between a well-read Eastern girl from Buffalo, New York, and a simple-living farm boy from South Dakota was forged.

Over the next year, Wit and Lucille worked diligently toward a goal of a wedding sometime in 1949. Wit worked on his father's farm and managed to find time to help Byrle with the farm that he and his wife Betty had purchased. Lucille waited tables and cooked at the Golden Pheasant Restaurant south of Spencer on Highway 38. By early summer, they realized that a wedding date of October 9, just nine days before Wit's 19th birthday was practical and affordable. Nearly 150 guests squeezed into the small Spencer Christian Church for the occasion. The newlyweds chose to forego a honeymoon until the following year and moved into a two-bedroom cottage on the west end of town. At the same time, Wit began steady employment driving a delivery truck for his brother-in-law Burle Matkins, who was married to his older sister Delma. Except for the death of Wit's grandmother, Bertha Schoepf, in the South Dakota State Hospital in Yankton, on November 22, Wit and Lucille's married life started nearly perfectly.

Shortly after New Year's Day in 1950, Lucille informed Wit that the second bedroom in their small house in Spencer would soon be claimed, probably in early or mid-July.

"Do you want a boy or a girl?' Lucille asked her husband.

"I don't know. What about you?"

"I hope it's a boy so you can have someone to play with all the time."
"What do you mean?" he asked quizzically.

"Wit Schoepf, you are the biggest kid I know, and I suspect you always will be," she answered with a smile.

Just after midnight on June 22, Lucille awakened Wit with the news that it was time to make the 15-mile trip to the nearest hospital in Canova. At 2:30 that morning, Michael Craig Schoepf made his screaming debut into the world. Wit had a playmate, but playtime would have to wait.

From the very beginning, Michael was a difficult baby. His entire body was as stiff as a clenched fist, he cried constantly and threw up half of his formula. For precautionary reasons, he was kept in the hospital for six days after birth. When his condition showed no improvement, Dr. Dick, the presiding doctor at the Canova hospital, recommended the baby be sent to Sioux Valley Hospital in Sioux Falls for testing and diagnosis. Wit drove silently while Lucille clutched little Michael closely.

Three days at Sioux Valley produced a diagnosis but not a solution. Michael was suffering from pyloric stenosis, a condition in which the opening from the stomach to the small intestine is abnormally narrow, preventing food from being processed as it should. Slowly, but steadily, the child was starving to death. The doctors there inserted an intravenous feeding tube in the inside of his left ankle to provide the child with much-needed nutrients and to prevent chronic dehydration. Their final recommendation was to take the baby to the University of Minnesota hospital in Minneapolis for more expert corrective surgery. Wit's father John and his mother Gay drove them so they could focus all their attention on their son.

On the second day in Minneapolis, doctors confirmed the original diagnosis and performed the life-saving corrective surgery. After a week in the Twin Cities, he was pronounced ready to go home with no condition-related restrictions.

Once back in Spencer, Wit returned to his truck driving job while Lucille stayed at home with Michael. Their life as a family seemed to be back on track, but that was short-lived. Medical bills began to pour in. As the amount they owed approached $5,000, they realized that Wit's weekly take-home pay of $33 and change wouldn't get them out of debt. That situation wasn't likely to improve, either. In February, Lucille informed her husband that another child would soon be joining the family. Clearly a change of finances was looming urgent. Lucille hinted at that in a telephone conversation with her mother early on a cold February night while Wit was practicing with his Spencer amateur basketball teammates.

The following evening, Lucille answered the telephone and recognized the voice as that of her father. Come to Buffalo, he said. Companies there are desperate for bright young men like Wit. They're even offering to pay for engineering training in order to have qualified help. Wit could probably have a well-paying job within a week. All he had to do to get one was show up. Lucille promised to talk to her husband about the idea before the conversation ended. Then she reluctantly awoke Wit from his customary early-evening nap. She was determined to approach the subject of moving almost 1,200 miles away with an infant and a baby on the way very carefully.

"O.K." was all Wit said after listening to her and taking less than a minute to think about the idea.

"Are you sure?"

"Why not? It sounds like a good idea. Besides, I've never been out of South Dakota except for last year. I'd kind of like to see more of the country. Let's go. On Sunday, we'll tell Mom and Dad."

As much as Wit embraced the idea of moving to Buffalo, his parents did not.

"You're going to do what?" Gay asked incredulously over Sunday dinner at the Schoepf farm. Wit's father John just sat in typical German stoic silence as the story unfolded.

"We're moving to Buffalo," Wit repeated.

"For heaven's sake, why?" Gay asked.

"Ma, we just can't get by on what I make here. We have too much in medical bills to pay, and, with another baby on the way, I don't see how we can ever get caught up. You, of all people, should know what that's like. When I took sick years ago, I know it took you and Dad years to pay off the doctors and hospital." Wit was referring to the time he was nine years old and was stricken with rheumatic fever. He had had a sore throat that wouldn't relent, followed by painful joints, a condition amplified because of his desire for constant activity. A week in the hospital, followed by two weeks of bed rest, was pure torture to him.

"It still doesn't make any sense," Gay continued. "Why not stay here at least until the baby is born? That way, you won't be traveling halfway across the country with a toddler and an expectant mother." The tone in her voice was an unmistakably disapproving.

"Mom, it's already decided. It's what we have to do." Wit said firmly to close the matter.

The next few weeks were a whirlwind of relocating activity for Wit and Lucille. They were generally too busy to care much that his mother was unusually cold to them. Finally, in the last week of April, they packed their Dodge and left Spencer, eastbound for Buffalo. Wit's parents were present to see them off, but the goodbye was awkward and not warm. Wit guessed that everyone was working to keep their true emotions in check.

Les Duly was right. The post-war economic boom was still alive and thriving in western New York. Within a week in Buffalo, Wit landed a mid-management job as a production scheduling engineer with Continental Can Company, a firm that manufactured industrial containers of all shapes, sizes and materials. Because he had no background in a manufacturing environment, the first six months on the job consisted of more training than actual production activity. He learned quickly and soon felt comfortable in the position. In the process, he learned that he was in the company of several equally inexperienced peers. Continental Can obviously believed in investing in potential.

On August 20, Lucille again informed Wit that the time to go to the nearest hospital was nigh. Later that day, Steven Dennis was born. Unlike his older brother, he was totally healthy. Wit now had two playmates. Steven was followed by Kevin in 1954, Susan in 1956 and Cindy in 1958. Also in 1958, Wit parlayed his successful experience at Continental Can into a more executive production engineer position with Sylvania Electric in Buffalo. He had also fulfilled Lucille's prophecy of being a playmate to his children.

Somehow Wit found time to play amateur baseball and basketball in the Buffalo area. He also made time to coach Mike and Steve in baseball. The left-handed Mike was a hard-throwing pitcher who worked to become an outstanding switch-hitter. Steve, like his father, was a natural shortstop with a gift for hitting a baseball and throwing a natural breaking curveball. Wit did little to hide his pride in his sons. The move to Buffalo was a good one. Wit and Lucille felt good about the road ahead for them and their family.

1961

Seven heads could be counted in the turquoise-and-white 1956 Chevy Bel-Aire parked outside McDonald's on West 12th Street in Sioux Falls on a muggy early-August day. In the driver's seat, Vinnie Healy was tallying up what he needed to order for his family's supper after an afternoon of shopping for supplies and clothes for the upcoming school year.   The trunk was full of pencils, pens, notebooks, crayons, dresses, socks, underwear and other miscellaneous items needed for academic attendance and success. Vinnie and his wife Toby could readily see that the day was one of their family's favorites.

With pen and notepad in hand, Vinnie began his survey. "How many want hamburgers?" he started. He noted that five hands went skyward.

"How many want cheeseburgers?" One hand went up. Counting himself, Vinnie wrote "2 cheese" on his list.

"French fries?" he queried. All hands rose. "7," he marked.

"How about chocolate shakes?" There were three takers. "

Vanilla shakes?" One.

"Coke?" Vinnie asked. Counting him, the result was three. Satisfied that he had a correct final tally, he left the car with his family trailing behind. Once their order was filled, he and two young girls carried their food to two adjoining tables and passed it out. It had been a great day, Vinnie reflected, a welcome break from his normal routine.

Not even in his most farfetched thoughts did Vinnie Healy ever think he would be raising the family he had. That it numbered six children did not surprise him. His father, Jim Healy, was one of ten children, and Vinnie himself was one of seven, all boys. That fact in mind, his family of one son and five daughters, seemed to defy mathematical odds. Daniel was born in June of 1947. Barbara, nicknamed Bobbie, joined the family in April of 1949. September of 1951 saw the addition of Beverly, dubbed Snookie. In November of 1952, Bonnie joined the clan, followed by Deanna in August of 1953 and Karen in September, 1958. Only Dan remained at home on this summer day. At 14, he was too old for that kind of thing, he had said.

Vinnie and Toby knew that their son was in the stage of life where he needed more than ever to express himself to establish his own identity and independence. Having once been teenagers themselves, they understood the transformation of Dan from boy to young man. Not having raised a teenager before, they weren't sure how to work with those changes.

In an effort to establish adult identity and to be of more help to his family, Dan pushed his parents for two weeks following his fourteenth birthday to take him to the courthouse in Salem to get his learner's driving permit. He reasoned with Vinnie and Toby that, if he were legally able to drive, something he had been doing on the farm for nearly five years, he could sometimes run errands that his busy parents found difficult to do. He was right, they agreed, so one morning, Vinnie took him to get the permit. A beaming young man, yellow permit in hand, returned before lunch. He likely didn't notice the pride in his parents' eyes. He was probably unaware, too, of how curious they were to see where he would lead them. It was a new adventure for all, with five more chapters to come.

As if raising teenagers weren't enough of a challenge, Vinnie and Toby Healy were facing another challenge of major importance. They both knew they would have to address it at some point, and that point had arrived. Important decisions with long-range effects could no longer be delayed.

No one knew math, particularly farm economics, better than Vinnie Healy. He knew how to manage the profits from a good year and how to maximize them from a lean one. He had an instinct for knowing when to sell crops and livestock for the highest price available. He also knew the value of setting aside money for future use. After all, he reasoned, something like the Great Depression could recur, and there would probably be expenses for replacement of machinery and possibly college educations for his children. He saw all those things in front of him and years behind him. There was one simple reason for that. He didn't own the land he depended upon to support his family.

Since 1947, Vinnie and Toby had rented their farm from his parents, Jim and Mary Healy, who had moved into Montrose. The rent had been fair and had only slightly increased in fourteen years. Still, Vinnie and Toby had no vested interest in the land. Though highly improbable, they and their children could be displaced at Jim and Mary's discretion. The fact that 71-year-old Jim and 67-year-old Mary were in the winter of their lives added urgency to finding some sort of resolution. Added to that was the fact that the farmhouse, almost eighty years old, was in need of some repair. It was badly in need of paint, new insulation and some new windows. Vinnie planned to talk with his parents about those things and the possibility of buying the farm from them as soon as the fall harvest was completed.

The harvest for the 1961 growing season was one of the better ones Vinnie had experienced. That was true for his brother Bus as well. Upon Bus's return from the army in 1953, the two Healy brothers were inseparable in helping each other. Even after Bus married and bought his own farm, they continued that arrangement. Though differing by five years and five miles, they had always found a way to get the work done, including machine maintenance and necessary repairs. 1961 was a typical year for the Healy brothers. In late November, the time for earnest discussion had arrived.

On the day after Thanksgiving, Vinnie and Toby drove to Montrose to take Jim and Mary to lunch at Fran's Café on Main Street. The plan was to treat the elder Healys to a meal they didn't have to prepare or clean up, then return to the house to discuss the long-range future of the Healy farm and the short-term of a house in need of some basic repairs. On the way back to the house, Vinnie brought up the reason for the visit.

"If you're not busy this afternoon, there's something we'd like to discuss with you when we get back to the house."

"Sure," his father replied. Upon returning to the house, Vinnie saw his mother start a pot of coffee, the large 30-cup one they had been given for their 40th wedding anniversary five years earlier. Just like Mom to sense this might be a long talk, thought Vinnie.

"So what do you want to talk about, son?" Jim asked. Vinnie looked at Toby to see her looking at him. He was sure her look said she was there to support him.

"Well, we've been doing some thinking and talking, Dad, and we wonder if you would be interested in selling the farm."

"To whom?"

"Us." For a long moment, Jim Healy didn't reply. Finally, he spoke.

"Why this sudden interest?"

"It's really not so sudden," Vinnie answered. "Toby and I started thinking about it several years ago."

"You didn't say anything before," Jim mused.

"It didn't seem so important until now," Vinnie countered. "Now our family situation has changed some, and the time seems right."

"How so?'

"Well, I just feel like we're caught in a tough spot right now. The house needs some work, and the barn needs repainting. We have the money to get those things done, but it's hard to justify spending it on buildings that aren't really ours." He paused to await his father's reaction. Jim merely sat at the table and rubbed his chin as he thought. Finally he spoke.

"What about your brothers? Have you spoken to any of them about this?"

"Only Bus, but I don't see why that matters. This would be just a simple real estate transaction. Why should they care?"

"Look, son, let me be clear. There are just two things that I want for that land. I want it always to be Healy land, and I want whoever works it to care for it as my father did, as I did, and as I see you doing. I know you were raised right, and so were your brothers.

I just think they should at least be aware of what we're talking about. What if one of them is interested in buying it?"

"I don't see why that would happen," Vinnie countered. "Joe, Bud and Bus have their own places. Gene is teaching in Utah, and Bob has his welding shop in town. Jerry is working road construction in Rapid." After a short pause, he added, "Besides, if you sold it, you could retire completely. You wouldn't have to sell any more seed corn, and you wouldn't have to come out to help Bus and me. Dan's old enough to do that. You and Ma could just relax or even travel if you wanted to."

"I like selling seed corn," Jim replied. He was referring to his unofficial reputation throughout McCook County and parts of Lake, Miner and Hanson counties as the "Corn King" who provided area farmers with the highest quality DeKalb seed corn. "And I like coming out to help you boys." His comments stalled the conversation at a stalemate. Finally Jim resumed the communication. "I have a solution to the house and barn problem."

"What's that?" Vinnie asked.

"Remember how I told you that the new interstate highway will be coming through the south end of the farm in the next year or two?" Vinnie nodded his head. "Well, the government bought a 150-foot wide strip of our land last month for a right-of-way. About 18 acres altogether. They paid me $100 an acre for it. So you'll have less farming to do next year. And I'll give you the money I got from the sale to fix up the house and repaint the barn. As for selling the land, I'll have to think on that for awhile. Suppose we talk about it again after Christmas." That ended the conversation. Vinnie knew it would be pointless to pursue the matter for the moment. He hadn't anticipated his father's resistance to the idea, and he wasn't prepared to counter it. He needed time to process what he had heard.

"I sure wasn't expecting to hear that," Toby said on the way home.

"Neither was I," Vinnie answered.

"What do we do now?"

"I guess we start looking for a farm to buy." Vinnie was sure he didn't want to do that, but he was equally sure he must.

"What if we don't find anything?" Toby wondered aloud.

"What if we do?" Vinnie wasn't sure which would be the more difficult predicament, leaving the family farm or feeling forced to stay there. As the situation played out, he didn't have to wait long to make a choice.

A week before Christmas, Vinnie found an ad in the county-wide classifieds in the *Canistota Clipper* offering 463 tillable acres of farmland four miles east of Spencer on Highway 38. The owner was planning to retire, and the land was to be sold separately from the machinery. An updated four-bedroom farmhouse was included. The house had running water and indoor plumbing, something the current Healy home did not. The asking price was $275 an acre, near the high end of the current market prices, but the size and stated condition of the house seemed to justify the cost. A little over $25,000 in down payment would be needed to secure the sale, an amount Vinnie and Toby had. In the short term, that amount would nearly drain their savings, but would give them the long-term financial security of owning their own farm. The house, too, was a significant upgrade, with enough room and modern conveniences for all. Vinnie picked up the telephone and called the listing real estate agent and made an appointment for him and Toby to see it the next day.

From the moment the Healys entered their prospective new home, Toby raved about nearly everything she saw. The front entryway opened into a spacious living room on the left and a formal dining room on the right. The dining room led to a large kitchen with an attached pantry and laundry room. A large mud room led outdoors from there. The living room displayed an open staircase to the second floor where the four bedrooms were located. Each had hardwood floors which had obviously been cared for and were partially covered in area rugs. The master bedroom was half again the size of their current one. In the center of the bedrooms was an open area with a wall of built-in drawers for storage and enough space to be a homework room. Vinnie was equally impressed with the house, but he was more interested in the barn, the other outbuildings and the land. He was not disappointed.

The barn and the outbuildings displayed the same amount of attention and care as the house. All had been painted the previous summer and Vinnie saw no gates, walls or fences needing repair. The barn had not been used for dairy cows in nearly twenty years and had never housed any beef cattle. Hence, it had been used only for hay and occasional machinery storage in that time. Still, he noted, it had been kept up meticulously. He climbed up to the hayloft to see how much of the 3/4 section he could see.

Seventeen acres of the ¾ section were deemed untillable. That included the house, he knew. The other unusable acres, the realtor said, consisted of a slough and a tree stand just north of the house. From what he could see, the workable land seemed as good as any he had seen. With a favorable viewing of the house, outbuildings and land fresh on their minds, the Healys set out for home to make a decision.

"I just love that house," Toby said to begin the discussion. "It has everything we need, and it's in such good condition. I could easily feel at home there."

"The land and buildings are in good shape, too," Vinnie added. "In fact, the buildings are just like new."

"Can we afford it?" Toby asked.

"Sure. It would be like starting over financially but with more than we had when we got married. The question is, 'Do we want to do that?'"

"Bus couldn't help you out anymore. We'd have to count more on Dan for the next several years." Toby remarked. "Can we do that?"

"I don't know," Vinnie replied. "Sometimes he sounds like he wants to stick around after high school and sometimes he seems like he has one foot out the door and no time to wait. The girls have turned out to be pretty good farmers, though."

"We also have to think about paying for some college educations, too," added Toby. "And I just realized that the kids would have to change schools. That's something I never had to do, did you?"

"Only when I went from country school to Montrose."

"Was it hard?"

"Not really. I already knew some of the kids from church."

"That wouldn't be the case for our kids, you know."

"I guess you're right. That's something we need to think about." They promised the realtor they would think about the property and told him they would call him shortly after Christmas."

For the next ten days, almost nothing else occupied Vinnie's thoughts. Everything about moving seemed right. Almost nothing about staying felt like a good idea. The kids would adjust, he thought. Kids do that, perhaps even better than adults. He would also have a title to land as collateral to do whatever he needed to do financially. The timing seemed right. At thirty-six, he was still young enough to control his and his family's future. Two days after Christmas, he picked up the telephone. He and Toby had reached a decision.

"Hi, this is Vinnie Healy. Toby and I have talked it over a lot and we're decided to stay where we are for now. Thanks for your time."

1964

Wilferd "Wit" Schoepf watched his wife Lucille usher their six children into the living room of their rented house at 21 West Islay Street in Santa Barbara, California. The day had been uncharacteristically cloudy in southern California. Wit hoped his message wouldn't be. He was glad Lucille was there to help him present it.

Lucille, Wit knew, was much better than he was at dealing with their children in the face of upsetting news. After all, she knew them better than he did. As a stay-at-home wife and mother, she was totally familiar with their differing personalities, even that of three-year-old Dan, who had joined the family in 1961 in Aurora, Colorado. Wit was sure he would need her help this evening and in the days to come.

"Kids," Wit began. "You all know, I think, that my health hasn't been the greatest lately." He was referring to the fact that an old nemesis, the rheumatic fever he had suffered as a nine-year-old on his parents' farm in South Dakota had come back to haunt him in the form of a defective and steadily deteriorating heart valve. Two cardiology specialists in Santa Barbara had pronounced him unfit to continue working. He then negotiated a severance package with American Machine and Foundry, his employer of the past three years. AMF, whose work in Titan missile bases such as Vandenberg Air Force base near Santa Barbara, was nearing completion, was more than fair with him. He had served them faithfully and capably as a production scheduling engineer and was scheduled for transfer to Little Rock, Arkansas. For that reason, they agreed to provide six months' pay, including accrued vacation time, and six months of health insurance coverage. The health insurance was vital. It would cover the costs of whatever medical attention he needed, and more. Lucille was expecting another child in October. The only thing left to decide was where he and his family would go.

"Go" is something that Wit and Lucille and their children had done almost constantly in the previous four years. After leaving suburban Buffalo, New York, for Aurora, Colorado, they lived in a rented house for a year and another one for a year. After leaving Sylvania Electric for a position with AMF, Wit was transferred to Santa Barbara, where the pattern of renting a home for a year, followed by moving into their current one, continued. Each move, Lucille told her husband, was mentally draining, physically exhausting and emotionally stressful. Still, they concluded that each was necessary.

"Because of that," Wit continued, "Your mother and I have decided to move again." He paused to study their faces for a reaction. On one of them, he saw a potential problem. Fourteen-year-old Mike was obviously unhappy with what he had just heard.

"Where are we going?" asked Susan, all of seven at the time. She was the one who shared Wit's curiosity about what was around the next corner or over the hill looming ahead.

"Well," Wit said, "we're going to South Dakota to see Grandma and Grandpa Schoepf in Sioux Falls." Wit's parents had sold their farm in Spencer and moved to Sioux Falls when Wit's younger brother Don finished high school and joined the army. Not having any sons around to help pretty much killed off any enthusiasm John had left for farming. Once in the state's largest city, he took a job as a custodian at Sioux Valley Hospital. The rift that had started when Wit and Lucille, along with Mike, left South Dakota for Buffalo, had been healed by time. Thirteen years has a way of doing that, Wit once thought.

"When are we going?" Susan continued. Always the one with all the questions, her parents had learned. She was sure to bring other inquiries with her on their journey.

"In about a week," was the answer she got. In that instant, Mike rose from the sofa and left the room. Wit started to follow him, but Lucille placed a hand on his forearm to stop him.

"Do they have fishing?' Steve asked. His father assured him that South Dakota did indeed have fish. Steve followed that question with another.

"Do they have baseball?'

"Yes, they do." Wit said. "In fact I played on a baseball team there when I was just a little older than you are." That answer seemed to satisfy the 12-year-old. Within a few minutes, it seemed that everyone's questions had been answered. Wit then prepared himself to talk to his oldest child. As he rose to go to Mike's room, Lucille again stopped him.

"Let me do it," she said. The firm tone in her voice convinced him. He sat down in his favorite stuffed chair, glad to know that most of his children would at least not be resisting the change of location.

Half-an-hour later, Wit saw Lucille come out of Mike's room. He studied her face for any clue of the outcome of her conversation with Mike. When he could see none, he asked her what happened.

"He said he's tired of changing schools all the time," Lucille replied. He was right, Wit knew. Counting two elementary schools in Buffalo, Mike would be entering his sixth school in nine years.

"He also told me he's sick of having to constantly make new friends every year, only to be ripped away from them at the end of the school year. He has some here that he doesn't want to give up."

"Did you tell him we plan to stay in South Dakota?" Wit asked.

"No. He probably wouldn't believe that anyway."

"So where are we at with him?"

"I told him that we need him to help out with the younger ones and to take on some adult responsibilities to make this work."

"Did he agree?"

"Reluctantly."

Two days later, Wit Schoepf sat in a bleacher seat behind home plate of the baseball field at Washington Elementary School in Santa Barbara watching the Bruins, his sons' team play for the city-wide midget league baseball championship. Leadoff hitter and shortstop Steve contributed three singles and a run scored, along with a diving catch of a line drive to his team's effort. Mike was the starting pitcher and pitched a complete game 4-1 win. Two of those four runs resulted from homeruns he hit off Ricardo Guzman, the second best pitcher in the league. After the game, Wit saw Freddie Daniels, the Bruins' coach stop Mike and Steve and talk them for a moment. Then he approached their father with a puzzled look on his face.

"I thought I had some good news for the boys," Daniels said. "But they don't seem to be too happy about it."

"What's that?" Wit asked.

"I just told them that they made the city league all-star team and we would be playing the Montecito all-stars in two weeks at Dodger Stadium in L.A. Neither of them seemed happy about it. In fact, Mike seemed to be on the verge of tears. What's going on?"

"Unfortunately, we're going to be moving to South Dakota. And the lease on our house is up at the end of next week, so we can't stay beyond that."

"Too bad," the coach replied. "They're both very good ballplayers. I've enjoyed working with them this summer." Then he turned and left. Swelled with fatherly pride, Wit also realized at that moment that good news sometimes makes a difficult situation worse.

As with most large families, the Schoepfs' 1,800-mile cross-country trip from Santa Barbara to Sioux Falls was a delightful, stressful, exciting and boring voyage all at once. Not surprisingly to Wit, Susan's first "Are we there yet?" was blurted out within the Santa Barbara city limits. "I have to go real bad," was also heard on many occasions, usually shortly after the previous restroom stop. Occasional outbreaks of flatulence sparked many stimulating conversations. The guilty party, of course, never confessed.

Four days later, after nighttime stops in Tonopah, Nevada, Little America, Wyoming and Rushville, Nebraska, Wit and Lucille's 1958 Pontiac Chieftain station wagon pulled up in the driveway of a house at 541 S. Glendale Avenue in Sioux Falls. Gay Schoepf, Wit's mother, greeted the adults with enthusiastic hugs and the children with kisses as well. The children were so glad to get out of the turquoise and white home on wheels that they didn't seem to mind. They would wash off the lipstick later.

Wit and Lucille were surprised to discover that four adults and seven children, including Wit's youngest sister Deanna, 17 years old, could co-exist in a two-bedroom ranch-style house for two weeks. During that time, Wit, Lucille and Dan were assigned to Deanna's bedroom while Deanna, Susan and Cindy were housed in the basement, the coolest place of all in the mid-July heat. Mike, Steve and Kevin slept in the partially finished attic with a ventilation fan and two large pedestal fans to keep them cool through the night.

During the day, Wit and Lucille studied and visited several options to house their family. Without an immediate income, they wanted to be as frugal as possible so their limited funds would last as long as they could be stretched. They also wanted to remain in or close to Sioux Falls so that the medical attention Wit would require would be convenient. Therein was the dilemma. As a city with mushrooming population growth due to the recently completed intersection of Interstates 90 and 29 on the northwest corner of the city, housing prices were as high as they were in California. Seems every landlord in the city had designs of cashing in on the future boomtown economy of the city. Wit and Lucille began to explore options in towns outside but near Sioux Falls.

Two weeks later, Wit and Lucille had found a solution to their housing crisis. All that remained was to tell Gay where they were about to move and to notify the moving company where to deliver their belongings. Wit expected his mother to rejoice in the news that her wayward son had finally come home to stay. He remembered the tense confrontation of thirteen years earlier when he told her that he and his family were moving to Buffalo, New York. He was wrong.

"You're moving WHERE?' Gay asked, probably hoping she hadn't heard correctly the first time.

"Montrose." Wit said, referring to a small town about thirty miles west of Sioux Falls.

"You can't do that!"

"Why not?" the younger Schoepf asked.

"You have a teen-age son and one about to be a teenager, don't you?' Gay pointed out.

"Yes. So?"

"That's a Catholic town."

"So?" Wit remembered Montrose from his truck driving days for his brother-in-law just after he and Lucille were married. One of the stops on his weekly route had been St. Patrick's Church to deliver cases of communion wine.

"It's full of Catholic girls! You know what they're like, don't you?" Wit knew his mother was referring to the Roman Catholic Church's official position opposing contraception and to the belief that the church was interested in having as many practicing followers as possible, either by conversion or conception. Apparently Gay was worried about both possibilities. Wit knew that his two oldest sons were in the next room and had probably overheard the entire conversation. He wondered how the idea of living in a Catholic community would set with them. He imagined Mike would be smiling, something he hadn't done in weeks.

Four days later, Wit and Lucille Schoepf moved their children into a two-story stone house on the south end of

Montrose. The house was owned by Bill Gustaf, the town barber and was one of several that he owned for rental income throughout the town. In order to create an extra bedroom, a local carpenter was retained to add a wall to an oversized bathroom upstairs. Wit planned for Mike to have the newly created room. It might soothe his son's feelings about having to endure another change of address, he thought. Steve, Kevin and Dan were assigned to one of the remaining upstairs bedrooms, and Susan and Cindy got the remaining one. Wit and Lucille would sleep downstairs, away from any potential chaos.

Settling in had barely happened when school began in the last week of August, a full week before California schools opened. Before long, Mike was staying after school for football practice and Steve and Kevin were pulling northern pike from the Vermillion River that ran by the east side of town. Susan and Cindy also found things of interest to do, and Dan kept Lucille occupied.

On October 15, Wit hurriedly ushered Lucille to Sioux Valley Hospital in Sioux Falls so that Sandra Joan could safely make her entrance into the world. Wit remembered Mike volunteering to stay home from school to care for Dan and watch Game 7 of the World Series between Steve's favored New York Yankees and his father's beloved St. Louis Cardinals. Wit was doubly delighted at the end of the day. Not only did he have a new healthy daughter, but the Cardinals won, 7-5 behind the competitive spirit of pitcher Bob Gibson. While staying with Lucille in the hospital, Wit decided the time had come for him to find a doctor in Sioux Falls to monitor his heart issues. Again, good fortune blessed him when he became a patient of Dr. Richard Braithwaite.

Wit learned instantly to trust Dr. Braithwaite. The doctor had a habit of explaining medical issues in layman's terms and freely added information about causes, risks and possible remedies. It was the latter category that he caught Wit's attention on only the second visit.

"You've been told, I'm sure, that this defective valve isn't likely to last much more than ten years or so." Wit nodded acknowledgement. "There may be a solution that could buy you another ten years or more beyond that." The doctor then stopped his prodding and poking long enough to look at Wit to make sure he had his patient's attention. He did.

"What's that?" Wit asked.

"Well, I was just reading last month about a group of doctors at the University of Minnesota hospital who have just started replacing parts of the human heart with artificial components, like plastic valves. Their hope is to someday be able to replace an entire human heart, but for right now, they're just working with valves. I think that, with your overall fitness, except for that pesky valve, you would be an outstanding candidate for a procedure like that." Again, he paused.

"How do I find out?"

"Let me make a phone call or two. I know one of the doctors in the group, and the lead surgeon, C. Walton Lillehei, is someone I met at a seminar a couple of years ago. What do you think?"

"Twenty years is better than ten," Wit replied. "Let's give it a shot."

A week later, Wit received a call from Dr. Braithwaite that the procedure was a "go". The Schoepfs had a week to make arrangements for housing their six children and to be in Minneapolis for the surgery. They made some phone calls to relatives and placed Susan, Cindy and the newborn Sandi with Wit's sister Delma in Spencer. Steve, Kevin and Dan would stay with Lucille's uncle Jean in Spencer while Mike would stay home in Montrose, watched over by the neighboring Boysen family.

Upon arrival at the University of Minnesota hospital, Wit was given a thorough physical examination which took nearly an entire day. Afterward, he was informed that the proposed surgery would be done the following day and would require approximately seven hours to complete. He knew it would be a long seven hours for Lucille, so he wanted to spend the evening bolstering her confidence. Have faith, he told her. After all, this is the same hospital that saved our son. Together, they made reassuring phone calls to speak to each of their children.

At 7:00 a.m. the following day, Wit Schoepf was anesthetized and wheeled into a surgical room. At 1:30 p.m., he was moved into the post-operative critical care ward while Dr. Lillehei informed Lucille that the procedure was successful. Barring any complications in the recovery process, Wit would be ready to go home in about two weeks. That evening, Lucille made another round of phone calls.

By mid-December, Wit was home in South Dakota and feeling just good enough to enjoy his favorite time of year, Christmas season. Despite growing up during the Great Depression when Christmas was not a lot of fun for many, Wit had always liked it. Presents were nice, he thought, but the spirit and decorations of the season were just as much fun for him. That's why he planned to take his children to Sioux Falls one evening to drive down Day Lane on the east side of town, dubbed "Candy Cane Lane" for the holiday season because of all the lighting displays erected by residents there.

On New Year's Day, 1965, Wit Schoepf realized that he, too, had finally found home and settled in. Ironically, it was the same state he couldn't wait to leave thirteen years ago.

In January, Mike Schoepf was reading his weekly U.S. history lesson, a chapter about how the Homestead Act of 1862 had affected the Great Plains, including South Dakota, when he realized the reason for something that had nagged him for 2 ½ years. Mike acquired his interest in history from his uncle, Dr. Leslie Duly, his mother's brother, who was currently a professor of history at the University of Nebraska in Lincoln. Mike was particularly interested in U.S. history. He liked to visit historic sites and to imagine the events that had occurred there. He also liked to know the reasoning behind those events. He knew, for example, that every town in the country came into being for a reason. Something motivated the first settlers to put down roots and establish the makings of a community.

Since moving to South Dakota in 1964, Mike had learned that cities like Sioux Falls originated because of its abundant water supply and it was the location of Fort Sod, an original military outpost on the prairie. Canistota was an early land office location. Salem, being the geographical center of McCook County and the intersection of two railroad lines, was a natural population center, commercial hub and county seat. Montrose had no such allure. In other words, some towns existed because they wanted to. Montrose, on the other hand, existed because it had to. In granting the right-of-way to the railroad, the federal government had stipulated that a tract of land be designated as a town site every ten miles or so. More people would be inclined to populate the region if they knew they would never be far from a town. That was the government's way of encouraging settlement. Hence, about halfway between Humboldt, another dribble of a town, and Salem, was Montrose, a community with no particular identity. Or so Mike thought when he arrived in August of 1964.

Mike's awakening started on his first Saturday in Montrose. Just after supper, he was sitting on the front porch of the stone house talking to a neighbor boy, Jim Boysen. Jim's family had previously lived in Spencer, as had Mike's parents, so a friendship between Mike and Jim took early root. After a few minutes mulling over the evening's entertainment possibilities, Jim suggested that they go downtown. Not really knowing the purpose of such an excursion, Mike agreed to make the four-block walk.

Mike expected to see the same quiet, relaxed downtown Montrose he had seen on his couple of daytime visits during the previous week. He was awed by what he saw instead. The streets were freely used by a number of cruising cars and pickup trucks. Numerous people were on the sidewalks. Both restaurants, Fran's and the Rosemont Hotel Café, were full of people. Many folks, farmers, judging by their attire, leaned on pickups talking idly. The repetitive dinging of the gas pump alerts at each of three gas stations filled the air. Two grocery stores seemed at maximum busy level as well. The most populated buildings seemed to be the pool hall and the neighboring municipal bar. All of these sights were foreign and pleasing to a newcomer from California.

For nearly an hour, Jim Boysen and his new sidekick wandered among the activity with Jim frequently stopping to talk to people. On every occasion, he introduced Mike. All of them, Mike noted, immediately and seamlessly included him in their conversations as if he had been living there for years. This might not be such a bad place after all, he thought.

Sports, especially baseball, had always been Mike's primary transition tool in a new environment. Talk sports, he knew, and social doors would open. Play sports and you would be welcomed inside those doors. Baseball season was over for the year in

Montrose, and the high school football team was just beginning its pre-season practices, so Mike joined the team. He had been a running back on the eighth-grade team at La Cumbre Junior High in Santa Barbara, so he knew what to expect. Again he was in for a surprise regarding life in a small town.

After the first day of practice, Mike was tired and sore. He hadn't experienced much physical activity in the month since baseball season ended in Santa Barbara, so he expected the fatigue and aching. As he trudged across the parking lot by the locker room to begin the five-block walk home, a black Chevy Impala stopped beside him. The driver's window rolled down and Mike recognized the driver as Glenn Jorgenson, the starting running back for the varsity team. He was also first-team All Corn Belt Conference Mike had heard.

"Like a ride there, California boy?" After a few seconds of stunned silence, Mike replied.

"Sure," he finally said. He walked around the car and got in the passenger side.

Instead of taking Mike directly home, Glenn drove around the town for awhile. "Driving around helps me relax after practice or a game," he said. "I hope you don't mind. How'd you get to be a running back?" Glenn asked.

"Last year in California, the coach told me he needed someone to play the position, mostly to block for the quarterback to run."

"Any good at it?"

"At the blocking, yeah. But for running, I was just fast enough to get the ball but not fast enough to get very far with it." Glenn laughed easily at that remark.

For twenty minutes or so, Glenn drove and asked Mike numerous questions about life in California. By the time he dropped Mike off at home, Mike realized that, even though he had done most of the talking, he gained far more information than he had imparted. Subsequently, he learned that riding around in cars was the South Dakota version of social media. It was the teenage thing to do, and it didn't generally matter who was riding with whom. The driver might be Big Tom O'Hara in his sporty new Mustang, or Roger Joachim or Kevin Kappenman or any of countless others. Years later Mike would realize that the subject matter of the conversations in cars differed, but, in the end, it was always about people.

After numerous knee issues, Mike Schoepf gave up football, leaving him with basketball and track as high school athletic endeavors. Baseball was not school-sponsored but offered through the local American Legion post, so he still had that. He also had another passion that had helped him in the past to adjust, academics. To the pride of his mother and her brother, he had little difficulty earning a spot on the honor roll, sometimes with little effort whatsoever. By the time his senior year at Montrose High School started in August of 1967, Mike was comfortable in the lifestyle the community offered.

Even though Mike could no longer play football, he planned to attend every MHS game that year. The team looked strong and could possibly defeat arch rival Freeman for the conference championship. In the pre-season polls, Montrose was rated #4 in the state and listed among its stars #16, defensive back Steve Schoepf.

In the home game against Bridgewater in October, Mike was standing near the bleacher seats on the home team side when something caught his eye. The football team looked overconfidently lethargic on the field, but the person in the leprechaun costume as the Irish mascot was way too hyperactive to ignore. At times, she was a better show than the one on the field. He recognized her as Beverly Healy, who had been Steve's same-height graduation marching partner at the end of their eighth grade year. In the two-and-a-half years since, Steve had grown some. Bev hadn't. Her enthusiasm in her duties as mascot seemed boundless, and he commended her for it. When she thanked him for the compliment, he was mesmerized by the most magnetic blue eyes he had ever seen. They lit up her freckles and contrasted her bright red hair beautifully. After that brief initial exchange, he found reasons to engage her in conversation at every opportunity. By evening's end, he had asked her for a date to the following week's game in Freeman. She accepted.

On Friday night the trip to Freeman was uneventful. The football game was well-played. The Irish won to preserve their perfect record. Halfway back home, the excitement began. What started out as a soft rumble in the left front of the car turned into a wheel wobble. Mike slowed to thirty miles per hour, causing them to arrive in Montrose at 11 o'clock. The car didn't worry him as much as the idea that she would be late arriving home and cause her mother to forbid her from seeing him. Fortunately, her sister Bobbie was still in town to take her home and neither suffered the wrath of an irate mother. On Saturday, Mike had the broken wheel bearing replaced and recalled that car trouble had brought him and Bev together once before.

The previous summer, Bev and Bobbie had come to town for summer band practice which was held on Wednesday nights. They had agreed to swing by and provide a ride for a friend. As they reached Montrose, Bobbie noticed that a tire was going flat. She drove immediately to the gas station owned by Mike's parents. While Mike's father repaired the ailing tire, Bobbie stayed, and Mike drove Bev to their friend's house to provide the needed ride. As the service station mechanic worked on Saturday morning to resolve the broken wheel bearing issue, Mike hoped that car repairs would not rule the new relationship he was enjoying.

Within a couple of weeks, Mike realized that weekends were too short and too long. They were short enough that the quality time he spent with someone whose pixie-like charm occupied most of his thoughts passed all too quickly. They were long enough that he missed seeing her between Saturday night and Monday morning in school. Bev quickly offered a solution. Each Sunday morning after Mass, her family would go to her grandmother's house next to the church for coffee and a week's worth of catch-up visiting. That would allow her nearly an hour to spend with him, so he started the custom of driving by the church just as Mass was dismissing. When she saw his white Ford Fairlane, she would jump in the passenger side and immediately slide toward him. Her uncle Bus, upon seeing that seating arrangement, commented that the car must only be half-paid for because only half of it was used.

In November, Bev invited Mike to Thanksgiving dinner at the Healy farm. He felt instantly elated then nervous. He had met Toby and Vinnie Healy in passing as he picked her up for dates but had never spent extended periods of time in their company. He didn't have a farm background, so he was afraid he had nothing in common to discuss with Vinnie. He also knew that Toby kept close tabs on her daughters and whom they were dating. The impression he got at first was that not every guy was good enough to date a Healy girl. The fourth Thursday in November would be his audition.

"So what do you plan to do after graduation?" Vinnie asked him as the dishes of food were being passed around the table.

"I'm going to go to USD," he replied, referring to the University of South Dakota, which Bobbie was already attending. "I plan to be an English teacher." That idea was largely influenced by his favorite teacher, Joe Haugen, who doubled as English teacher and guidance counselor at Montrose High. The rest of the afternoon followed the same agenda. Vinnie would ask questions about Mike and his family and Mike would answer them in as relaxed a tone as he could muster. He noticed that Toby listened carefully to each answer as if measuring it, but she offered little clue about what she was thinking.

In late afternoon, Bev walked Mike out to his car. She held his hand and showed him a smile that lit up the dusky autumn sky. He noticed that even in the near dark, her crystal blue eyes held him helplessly captive.

"Relax," she said. "I think you passed the parent test."

"How do you know?"

"I asked Mom if I could invite you to midnight mass for Christmas, and she said that was alright with her."

"What about your dad? He sure had a lot of questions."

"Oh, don't worry about him. If he didn't like you, he wouldn't have been so interested." With that, she gave him a quick kiss on the cheek and turned to walk into the house. "See ya' tomorrow night," she said, referring to their movie date for the following evening. He watched her enter the porch, then drove home smiling.

By the time spring planting season arrived, Mike knew he had scored points with Bev's father. Vinnie asked him if he wanted to earn some extra money on days he wasn't scheduled to work at the gas station. Vinnie and Bus could use some help disking the fields they farmed to prepare them for seeding. When he told Vinnie he had never driven a tractor before, Vinnie assured him that he would show him how to do that. Only a courageous and trusting person would trust a beginner with a $100,000 piece of farm machinery, Mike concluded. That meant that he had obviously scored some serious "Dad" points.

In August of 1968, Mike entered USD, knowing that his relationship with Bev would face its most difficult test yet. For the first time since they started dating, they would be separated for days at a time. That weighed heavily on him. He had grown very dependent on her company. He missed her. He had come to count on her for inspiration to be the best person he could be and for emotional support in trying times. That could only mean one thing, he reasoned. He was in love.

That fall, Mike and Bev began to talk seriously of a future together. He would finish college, they decided. Then he would find a job teaching high school English. They would have at least one child, a son named Ryan Michael, and live in a nice home somewhere so she could be a stay-at-home housewife and mother.

Mike's baseball experience taught him that sometimes life throws curveballs at people who are expecting fastballs. Mike and Bev were geared up for a heater when their plans suddenly changed direction. To begin with, Mike announced that he didn't particularly like USD. He said he didn't feel comfortable in classes that had 100 or more students in an auditorium, unlike the 30 or so he had experienced at Montrose High School. He told her he intended to transfer to Dakota State College in Madison, only half as far away as Vermillion, home of USD. He also explained that Madison offered more job opportunities for him to work while he attended classes. He wanted to be financially self-sufficient, he explained. After all, his parents had seven other children to support since Cathleen had been born on Valentine's Day in 1966.

Bev agreed with Mike's plan. She added that, as a senior in high school, she was planning to take her high school diploma somewhere, probably Sioux Falls, to find clerical work and begin to save money as a stake for their future. Again, their agenda seemed in order and working. In fact, by the summer of 1970, Bev was working as a directory assistance telephone operator for Northwestern Bell in Sioux Falls, and they bought a car, a blue 1964 Ford Falcon Futura, together. The time to take the next step had arrived. Timing was somewhat of a concern. Bobbie had just married Tom Spicer of Canistota in September. Later that month, in the living room of the Healy family farm in Canistota Township, with her approving family as witnesses, Mike Schoepf proposed to Beverly Healy. She accepted.

Mike's parents took the news in contrasting fashion. Wit responded with "It's about damn time!" Lucille, on the other hand, asked immediately if that meant that Mike would not be completing his final year-and-a-half of college. Assured that he would indeed earn his degree, she was still skeptical. Mike told her that they would be living in Sioux Falls and he would be driving 50 miles to Madison and back each day for classes. When she still did not seem happy, the engaged couple chalked up her reaction as being an overprotective mother. She saw the idea as losing a son rather than gaining a daughter. Mike and Bev agreed to not concern themselves with her response to their news. There was much to be done and little time in which to do it. To himself, Mike made a promise to prove his mother wrong. He couldn't afford not to.

1971

On Saturday, January 16, the sun shone brightly, making for a radiant, crisp winter day in eastern South Dakota. No snow was forecast until the following day. At 1:00 p.m. in St. Patrick's Catholic Church in Montrose, South Dakota, Father Patrick O'Connor presided over the wedding of Beverly Katherine Healy and Michael Craig Schoepf. Sandi and Cathi Schoepf, the youngest of the Schoepfs, were the flower girls. Nearly two hundred family members and friends witnessed the event. Year-and-a-half old Amy, Bev's youngest sister, was among the crowd. After almost 120 years, two paths with kindred origins had finally merged.

Thank You To...

My mother, Lucille Schoepf, who instilled in me a love of reading, writing and a lifelong sense of optimism.

My father, Wilferd Schoepf, who left me a notebook of memories and the knowledge that it's o.k. to never grow up.

My father-in-law, Vincent Healy, and my mother-in-law, Virginia Healy, for providing me with information I needed to make this story complete and, most important, giving me the greatest gift I could ever want.

My sister, Cathi, who taught so many people how to live and, just as important, how to die.

My paternal grandmother, Gay Schoepf, who left written memoirs of a truly remarkable life.

My late uncle, Dr.Leslie Duly, who reinforced the same communication lessons taught by his sister, my mother.

My father's late cousin Glenn, who, for decades acted as Schoepf family historian, and, thus compiled much of the factual information used in the telling of this story.

Historian Myra Voss, East Side Cemetery caretaker Frank Phippen and the entire staff of the Clayton County Recorder's Office, all of Elkader, Iowa. Their swift, gracious and smiling assistance made digging for facts a true joy.

My wife's aunt, Mary Healy, for her insights that brought some of the characters to life.

Michelle Eichacker, my wife's cousin, who gave me a significant missing piece of the Healy family story.

My nephew, Chad Spicer, for editing this story to help make it right.

To priceless neighbors George McCarthy and the late Harold Hanson, whose passion for looking for the stories behind the facts of genealogical research inspired me to see this project through to completion.

About the Author...

Michael Schoepf is a retired educator, newspaper executive and marketing consultant who was raised in each of the continental time zones, but mostly in South Dakota. He currently lives in Albert Lea, Minnesota, with his wife Bev and adult children Maria and Tony. In addition to *Sons of the Soil,* he previously published *Iron Mountain*, a story of how good people are sometimes caught up in unfortunate circumstances.

"*Iron Mountain* is a story I wanted to write," he says. "'*Sons of the Soil*'" is the story I was meant to write."

A lifetime of experience with various types of people has given Michael an understanding that helps him paint word pictures of the characters in his work. According to him, each is modeled on someone he knows or is a composite of two or more of the people who have been a part of his life.

Michael's next project is planned to be a series of essays based on his 16 years of experience teaching in a sheltered care youth group home. He is also considering writing a sequel to *Iron Mountain.* He can be contacted at *michaelschoepf1950@gmail.com*